A Handbook of Historical Briefs

Testimonies of learned historians, scholars, editors, and debaters on the history and beliefs of Baptists, the majority of whom are Baptists

By J. PORTER WILHITE

With An Introduction
By Thomas B. Warren

And a brief Biography
By H.A. "Buster" Dobbs

"One of themselves, even a prophet of their own, said."
—Titus 1:12

Charleston, AR:
COBB PUBLISHING
2021

A Handbook of Historical Briefs is copyright Cobb Publishing ©2021, all rights reserved. This document (whether in whole or in part) may not be reproduced in any way, whether digital, audio, print, or any other means, nor stored in any online system designed for sharing files without prior written permission from the publisher.

Published in the United States of America by:
Cobb Publishing
704 East Main St
Charleston, AR 72933
www.CobbPublishing.com
CobbPublishing@gmail.com
479-747-8372

BIOGRAPHY OF
J. PORTER WILHITE

It is a privilege to write a biography of the life of J. Porter Wilhite for use in this valuable book. Brother Wilhite is well known to all who have had an interest in the work of the church over the past four decades, for a period of forty-four years he has proclaimed the Good News of salvation, preaching his first sermon on a cold January morning at Friendship, Van Zandt County, Texas in the year 1910. Since that day, brother Wilhite has unselfishly dedicated himself to the work of the Lord.

J Porter Wilhite was born in Canton, Texas to John H. and Anna Wilhite. He was reared in Canton where he received a liberal education, finishing his educational work at the University of Houston.

Early in his career as a gospel preacher, brother Wilhite conducted a meeting at Jones School House, in Canton, Texas. The success of that first effort, which resulted at least in one gospel preacher) inspired him to go wherever opportunity offered. Brother Wilhite says, "My second meeting was under a brush arbor in near Grand Saline, with twenty-five baptisms in a one Sunday meeting. No doubt I would have baptized more, but had to close because I didn't know any more to preach at the time. They paid me $25.00, and I thought I would soon be rich."

Mattie Harrison became the devoted wife of brother Wilhite. To that union four children were born, all of whom still live. Sister Mattie Harrison Wilhite was tragically killed in an automobile accident in Arkansas while on route to join brother Wilhite. Her untimely death made an irreparable wound in the heart of her devoted husband, but instead of leaving him morose, cynical and bitter, this personal encounter with the pale visitor made brother Wilhite more understanding, more loving, more tender, and more determined to serve the Master.

Later, brother Wilhite accepted the invitation of the church at Munday, Texas to work with them as local evangelist. During his tenure at Munday, he married Alyce Whittemore, a widowed mother of three small children, who is still his loving and devoted wife.

He has done local work with the church at Munday, Bonham, Temple, Fort Worth, and Houston, Texas; also, Monroe, and Minden, Louisiana, and Anadarko, Guthrie, and Shidler, Oklahoma. A large part of his life has been spent in conducting gospel meetings on a nation-wide scale. He has recently returned from a five-week tour of the Northern part of the United States.

Brother Wilhite has defended the cause of Christ in about fifty public debates, meeting such outstanding Missionary Baptists as Drs. Albert Garner, J.E. Cobb, and D.N. Jackson; W.A. Hearron and I.W. Yandell, leaders of the

Free-Will Baptists; also Cannon and Welch, leaders of the Pentecostal denomination. Two of his debates are in print. Brother Wilhite has also written several successful tracts, viz., "Butting Kidd", a review of Methodist doctrine and a reply to a man named Kidd. "Operating on a Baptist Doctor, (No. 1,)" and "Operating on a Baptist Doctor, (No. 2.)" The first of these is a review of the work of Dr. J.W. Porter of fame among Missionary Baptists, and the second is a review of Dr. Albert Graner's little smear, "A Few Asperins For Campbellites."

Due, no doubt, to his frequent encounters with Baptist preachers, brother Wilhite began very early in life to study Baptist doctrine and history. For the last fifteen years, he has made church history a special study. His personal library is an outstanding collection of various histories, including those written by the very best scholars in the Baptist church. In all modesty, it may be safely said, that, in this field brother J. Porter Wilhite is an authority.

Brother Wilhite and his fine wife are presently engaged actively in the work of the Lyons and Majestic streets church in Houston, Texas, where he has been for the past three years, and where he formerly preached for almost six years; and where it is my happy privilege to be closely associated with this godly man. He is loved and esteemed by the brethren here, as he is loved and esteemed by all who know him.

H.A. [Buster] DOBBS,
An evangelist of the Church of Christ, under the direction of the elders of the Lyons & Majestic church in Houston, where brother Wilhite also works.

FOREWORD

Many different religious sects are now, as in the past, striving to gain the attention and allegiance of the public. Few surpass the Baptists in zeal at this particular point. That they have been successful in gaining the attention and allegiance of a great many is evident to all who bother to examine the evidence. Perhaps the appeal which they have used with the most telling force is their claim to be able io trace themselves through history back to the church of the New Testament. That this claim is eminently false is plainly evident to anyone who has a Bible and a few history books. Few men, however, have the books which would be necessary to check their claim. It was needful, therefore, that no one who did have access to such books make this information available to all so that all may see the falsity of Baptist claims on church succession. In presenting Historical Briefs to the reading public, J. Porter Wilhite has accomplished that very thing. In this book, brother Wilhite has put the historical information of a great many books, many of which or very difficult to obtain, at the very finger tips of the reading public. The price is so low as to be insignificant to those who realize the great amount of research which went into the production of this small book. I hope for it a very wide reading.

Thomas B. Warren
Galena Park, Texas
April 22, 1953

TABLE OF CONTENTS

Chapter 1 ORIGIN OF THE CHURCH 1
Chapter 2 BAPTIST CHURCH SUCCESSION 7
    MONTANISTS 7
    NOVATIANS 8
    DONATISTS 9
    PAULICIANS 10
    ALBIGENSES 11
    PETROBRUSIANS 12
    WALDENSES 13
    ANABAPTISTS 15
Chapter 3 ORIGIN OF MODERN BAPTISTS 17
Chapter 4 MODERN BAPTISTS HAVE CHANGED 24
    FOOT WASHING 25
    HAD ELDERS 25
    INSTRUMENTAL MUSIC 26
    REVEREND 26
    WEEKLY COMMUNION 27
    ASSOCIATIONS AND CONVENTIONS 27
    A BIG UNIVERSAL CHURCH 28
    JOHN'S BAPTISM 30
    THEY ONCE SAID ANY COULD DO THE
        BAPTIZING 31
    MARK 16:16 32
    NOW THEY SAY THE GREAT COMMISSION
        WAS GIVEN TO THE CHURCH, BUT THEY
        TAUGHT IT DIFFERENTLY 33
    EARLIER VIEWS OF THE BAPTISTS. 34
    THEY ONCE ACCEPTED BAPTISM FROM
        OTHER CHURCHES, EVEN THE
        DENOMINATIONS 34
Chapter 5 BAPTISTS IN AMERICA 37
    PROVIDENCE CHURCH 37
    NEW PORT CHURCH 38

Chapter 6 BAPTISTS IN AMERICA 46
    SOME OLD LETTERS 50
Chapter 7 BAPTISTS IN AMERICA 54
    THOMAS CAMPBELL 54
    ALEXANDER CAMPBELL 55
Chapter 8 BAPTISTS CLAIMED CAMPBELL 63
Chapter 9 HUMAN CREEDS 71
    ASSOCIATIONS 73
APPENDIX 80
    JOHN'S BAPTISM NOT THE SAME AS OUR
        BAPTISM 90
WHO IS WHO IN HISTORICAL BRIEFS? 94

CHAPTER 1
ORIGIN OF THE CHURCH

Speaking of the great day of Pentecost, we quote, "On account of this event, the Pentecost which the disciples celebrated soon after the Savior's departure, is of such great importance, as marking the commencement of the Apostolical church, for here it first publicly displayed its essential character. Next to the appearance of the Son of God himself on earth, this was the greatest event, as the commencing point of the new divine life, proceeding from him to the human race." (Augustus Johann Neander, Planting and Training of the Church, p. 18.)

"On the day of Pentecost, they became fully qualified, by the outpouring of the Holy Spirit, for rightly understanding and correctly executing their Lord's will... The extraordinary circumstances of the day of Pentecost... at which time Peter opened to the Jews the gospel system of salvation. Three thousand felt the force of truth... they arose, were baptized, and washed away their sins... This church of Jerusalem ... so constituted is the acknowledged pattern or model by which other Christian churches were formed, 1 Thess. 2:14: since 'the law was to go forth out of Zion, and the word of the Lord from Jerusalem.'... This Christian assembly as it was the first, so it is the mother church in the Christian dispensation." (G.H. Orchard, A Concise History of Foreign Baptists, pp. 5-7.)

"The Jewish Pentecost... received in the year of Christ' death (30) an immeasurable significance, as the birthday of the church and the beginning of the third era in the revelation of the triune God." (Philip Schaff, History of the Christian Church, p. 59.)

"The first Christian church founded by the apostles, was that of Jerusalem, the model of all those which were afterward erected during the first century." (Mosheim, Ecclesiastical History, Part 1, chap. 4, p. 12.)

"It was the birthday of the church, and its first members were won by the preaching of Peter to the wondering multitude." (Kurtz's History, trans. Macpherson, I, 40.)

"The almost universal opinion among theologians and exegetes is this: That Pentecost marks the FOUNDING OF THE CHRISTIAN CHURCH AS AN INSTITUTION. This day is said to mark the dividing line between the ministry of the Lord and the ministry of the Spirit." (Henry Dosker, New International Bible Encyclopedia, "Pentecost, '

"According to the accepted Chronology, these (the followers of Jesus) began their mission on the day of Pentecost, A.D. 29, which day is regarded, accordingly, as the birthday of the Christian church." ("Christianity," Catholic Encyclopedia.')

"In Jerusalem the new movement had its center, and the church established there is rightly known as the mother church of Christendom." (Encyclopedia Britannica, 14th Edition, V, 676.)

"The most notable Pentecost was the first which occurred after the resurrection and ascension of Christ (Acts 2). From it dates the founding of the Christian church." ("Pentecost," New Westminster Dictionary of the Church.)

"Constituted as Christ's mystical body on Pentecost; thenceforth, expanded in the successive stages traced in Acts." ("Church," Bible Cyclopedia.)

"The day of Pentecost is the birthday of the Christian Church. The Spirit, who was then sent by the Son from the Father, and rested on each of the disciples... combined them as they never had before been combined, by an internal and spiritual bond cohesion. Before they had been individual followers of Jesus, now they became his mystical body." ("Church," Smith's Bible Dictionary, p.161

"For the proclamation of this truth the church was the appointed agent; the story of Pentecost, therefore, is the first chapter in the history of the church." (Charles R. Erdman, The Acts: An Exposition, p. 28.)

"The day of Pentecost is the birthday of the Christian church. Before, they had been individual followers of Jesus; now they become his mystical body, animated by his Spirit. The REAL Church consisted of all who belong to the Lord Jesus Christ, as his disciples, and are one in love, in character, in hope in Christ, as the head of all, though as the body of Christ it consists of many members." (Peloubet's Bible Dictionary, p. 119.)

"John the Baptist... baptized the penitent for the remission of sins; but he organized no church among his disciples... The personal ministry of Jesus was preparatory to the constitution of churches. During his life no church was organized... On the day of Pentecost, after the ascension of Jesus, the apostles, by the descent of the Holy Spirit, were fully qualified to carry forward and complete the work that John and Jesus had begun. The first church was formed in Jerusalem, and this soon became the mother of other churches in various countries." (J.B. Jeter, Baptist Principles Reset, pp. 20-21.)

"Actual existence as an organized society of believers during the life of Jesus, no trace appears in the four gospels. The day of Pentecost marks the beginning of the definite, organic life of the followers of Christ." (Vedder, Short History of the Baptists, p. 14.)

"World-wide operation began there on the day of Pentecost." (Ben M. Bogard, Bogard-Borden Debate, p. 84.)

"Up to this time the preaching, with a few exceptions, was to be done by the disciples to Israelites in Palestine. The commission, therefore, was limited... But before our Lord ascended, he gave his church a world-wide commission... but the worldwide ministry of the church did not begin until the day of Pentecost had dawned." (D.N. Jackson, Holy Ghost Baptism, p. 12.)

"In the fulness of time Christ the King appeared; and his kingdom, after his earthly humiliation and suffering, was fully inaugurated at his ascension, when he was enthroned in heaven." (H. Harvey, The Church, p. 22.)

"Looking then for the birth of the church he finds (contrary, perhaps, to his expectations, for he has probably been taught that Adam and the Patriarchs are in the church) that it certainly did not exist before, nor during, the earth-life of Christ, for he finds him speaking of his church as future when he says (Matt. 16:18) "Upon this rock I will build my church'... Scripturally, he finds the birth of the church in Acts 2 and the termination of its career on the earth in 1 Thess. 4." (Dr. C.I. Scofield's tract, "Rightly Dividing the Word of Truth," p. 6.)

"THE BAPTIST CHURCH, as the church of Christ, has existed from the day of Pentecost to the privileged period." (D.B. Ray, Baptist Church Succession, p. 446.)

MATT. 16:18

"The Greek word is oikodomeso, and means, literally, 'I shall build'... Could not here mean 'Edify,' 'Embellish,' 'Build up'." (From a letter written by Dr. J.F. Paxton, University of Oklahoma.)

"The Greek word used in this passage is oikodomco, which means, 'I build.' In the future tense used in this passage it is oikodomeso, which means, 'I shall build.' These are Thayer's exact words: 'to build a house, erect a building; to build (up from the foundation).' I have neither added to, nor taken from Thayer's exact words. The above is the primary sense of the word." (From a letter written by Dr. L.T. Wallace, Department of Bible and Greek, Oklahoma Baptist University.)

"The word used here is from oikodomeso, in the future tense. Its literal meaning is to build a house... Thayer of Harvard, in his lexicon, gives it the literal meaning in this passage, and translates it, 'to found'." (From a letter written by Mrs. Helen Dow Baker, Hardin-Simmons University.)

"'Will build' is future form." (Dr. J.E. Cobb, Cobb-Wilhite Debate, p. 9.)

A Handbook of Historical Briefs

"Means 'to build,' in the sense one would speak of building a house. He certainly did not mean by the word to enlarge, embellish, or edify his church." (Letter written by Shaler Matthews, Chicago University.)

"It does not mean to enlarge, embellish, or strengthen a house already built; it simply means 'I will build'; ... it implies that the building was not yet done, but was to be done." (From a letter written by Gross Alexander, Vanderbilt University.)

"To translate them 'build' in this connection by 'enlarge' or 'embellish' would mar the metaphor and dilute the thought." (From a letter written by Professor Thayer.) (These last three are quoted by Joe S. Warlick in Baptist Blunders, p. 16.)

"To build a house, erect a building; to build (up from the foundation) ... by reason of the strength of thy faith thou shalt be my principle support in the establishment of my church, Matt. 16:18." (Thayer, Greek-English Lexicon, pp. 439-440.)

"He (Peter) was the leading preacher on the day of Pentecost, and the first to preach the gospel to the Jews, Acts 2:11; and to the Gentiles, Acts 10:1ff." (J.M. Pendleton, Brief Notes on the New Testament, p. 60.)

"I will build comes from a Greek word here meaning to edify, build up, etc., and not to found... (VERSE 18) JESUS CHARGES THE DISCIPLES THAT THEY TELL NO MAN THAT HE WAS THE CHRIST. (His Caps, J.P. W.) ... after his death and resurrection they could tell what wonderful things that they had seen the Lord do, etc., and thereby be eye-witnesses, in popular opinion, to the works, death and resurrection of Jesus Christ." (Dr. D.N. Jackson, Baptist Sunday School Senior Quarterly, Second Quarter, 1933.)

DEATH, BURIAL AND RESURRECTION "could not be used with full effect, until they had been accomplished." (Alvah H. Hovey, American Commentary, III, 314.)

"What is a church? ... a congregation of Christ's baptized disciples, acknowledging him as their head, relying on his atoning sacrifice for justification before God, and depending on the Holy Spirit for sanctification, united in the belief of the gospel." (J.M. Pendleton, Baptist Church Manual, p. 7.)

"But in the absence of penitent, regenerate, baptized believers in Christ, there cannot be a New Testament church." (Ibid., p. 15.)

SUMMING UP. Taking these definitions from the best authority Baptists have, one can see, since it takes belief in Jesus as a crucified, buried and raised Son of God, which they could not believe was a fact before it was accomplished; and since one had to be baptized by immersion in the name of the Father, Son and Holy Spirit in order to be in the Baptist church, which was never authorized until after Jesus was raised, as recorded in Matt. 28:19; and since He was made head AFTER being raised, Eph. 1:18-23, therefore, we conclude that there was no church that would satisfy the Baptists, or any one who teaches that it existed as a working body, before the resurrection. Even if there had been an active church then, it had no head such as we now have in the church, Eph. 1:18-23.

Chapter 2
BAPTIST CHURCH SUCCESSION

Ben M. Bogard's way of tracing the Baptist church succession goes like this: Apostolic Age; Montanists; Novatians; Donatists; Paulicians; Albigenses; Petro-Brusians; Waldenes; Ana-Baptists, and Modern Baptists. (Ben M. Bogard, Baptist Way-Book, p. 62.)

Since we cannot read about the Baptist church in the apostolic age, we will leave that for the friends of Baptist church succession to find the reason why it isn't in the Bible. We will content ourselves in tracing the people Dr. Bogard, the Baptist debater who claimed to have had more debates in defense of the Baptist church than any other who ever lived, says were good Baptists.

MONTANISTS

"Montanus, A.D. 156, like the people among whom he was reared, was fond of the marvelous and ecstatic... Divinations and clairvoyance were believed to be priestly endowments." (Hurst, Short History of the Christian Church, p. 44.)

"Montanus was charged with assuming to be the Holy Spirit himself; which was simply a slander. They excluded themselves from society . matter itself was an unmixed evil." (Armitage, History of the Baptists, pp. 175-176.)

WERE THEY BAPTISTS?

"The Montanistic prophets spoke with tongues, with accompaniments of ecstasy and trance... The revelations thus received by these prophets were held to be supplementary, and in a sense superior to the Scriptures." (Vedder, Short History of the Baptists, p. 59.)

"About A.D. 200, he (Tertullian) became a Montanist, among which sect he ranked as the leader, and at Carthage first launched his famous work on baptism against Quintilla who held that faith saves without baptism." (Armitage, op. cit., p. 174.)

"Not until we reach the twelfth century do we encounter types of Christian life that we can with any confidence recognize as Baptists." (Newman, History of the Baptist Churches in the United States, p. 13.)

NOVATIANS

"About A.D. 281, the Novatians arose ... he was supposed to lie at the point of death, and asked baptism in order to save his soul ... it was poured all over him till he was drenched, making perfusion as near an immersion as possible. If he died, this was to stand for baptism, saving him by a narrow escape; but if he lived, his baptism was to be considered defective... They reckoned that no man could be saved without being baptized." (Thomas Armitage, History of the Baptists, pp. 177-178.)

"The Novatian churches were what are now called Baptist churches, adhering to the apostolic and primitive practice." (J.M. Cramp, Baptist History, p. 59.)

"The character and disposition of Novatian, whose very pretensions to religion were all the works of the Devil. This wretch, fearing he was going to die, was sprinkled on his bed—if, indeed, it is fit to say that such a one (so depraved) received it." (D.B. Ray, Baptist Church Succession, p. 321.)

A BAPTIST?

"Novatian was an elder in the church at Rome... mark this, if you violate the contract by lapsing into idolatry or vice, we shall separate you from our community; and, do what you will, we shall never readmit you." (Benedict, History of the Baptists, pp.4-5.)

"They considered the baptism administered in those churches, which received the lapsed to their communion, even after the most sincere and undoubted repentance, as absolutely divested of the power of imparting the remission of sins." (Johann Lorenz Von Mosheim, Ecclesiastical History, p. 74.)

WERE THEY GOOD BAPTISTS?

"It (Novatians) lost strength, however, with the death of its leader, and in time went into decay." (Hurst, Short History of the Christian Church, p. 55.)

DONATISTS

"The Donatist agitation arose in North Africa, A.D. 311." (Armitage, History of the Baptists, p. 200.)

"No Baptist in modern times brands the accursed union between church and state with more appropriate condemnation than did his ancient Donatist brothers." (William Cathcart, The Baptist Encyclopedia, I, 342.)

"Walsh asserts that Constantine had condemned them in his decrees, before they appealed to him for the trial of their case." (Thomas Armitage, History of the Baptists, p. 201.)

"The Donatist party in Africa, like the Novatians in Rome, seemed to originate in a mere squabble over an office." (Vedder, Short History of the Baptists, p. 64.)

"The Donatist did not differ from the Catholics in doctrine." (Orchard, A Concise History of Foreign Baptists, p. 86.)

WERE THESE GOOD BAPTISTS?

"These Baptists descended from the Waldenses, whose historical line reaches far back and connects with the Donatists, and theirs to the Apostolical churches." (J.R. Graves, Trilemma, pp. 121-122.)

"Novatians and Donatists seem to have shared the errors of the Catholic church regarding sacramental grace;

their episcopacy cannot be distinguished from that of the Catholic church, and was certainly far from the simplicity of apostolic order. The Donatists, at any rate, seems to have practiced infant baptism." (Vedder, Short History of the Baptists, p. 66.)

WERE THESE GOOD BAPTISTS?

"Novatianists and Donatists were more insistent than the Western Catholics on the regenerating- efficacy of baptism and its applicability to infants." (A.H. Newman, A Century of Baptist Achievement, p. 2.)

GOOD BAPTISTS, EH?

PAULICIANS

"It was about the year 653, that a new sect came into notice in the East, under the name of Paulicians." (Orchard, A Concise History of the Foreign Baptists, p. 127.)

"They first appeared about 660 A.D." (Armitage, History of the Baptists, p. 237.)

"They rejected the perpetual virginity of Mary... neither were they Baptists." (Armitage, Ibid., p. 238.)

YOU SAY BAPTISTS?

"...were poor specimen of Christianity any way, when measured after the full order of the gospel. But the Christian world at that time afforded nothing better." (Armitage, Ibid., p. 239.)

"They have always been coupled with the Manichaeans, and nothing has been too base to say of them." (Armitage, Ibid., p. 234.)

"The Paulicians rejected water baptism." (Cramps, Baptist History, p. 79.)

"They did not accept the Mosaic writings as part of the word of God, though they did accept the Psalms and New Testament; they rejected water-baptism... they declared the

Lord's Supper to be the sacrifice of demons, and would have none of it; they thought churches the dwelling-places of demons... they forbade marriage and the eating of flesh, and fasted thrice a week." (Vedder, Short History of the Baptists, p. 77.)

WERE THEY GOOD BAPTISTS?

"Some Baptist writers have sought to find in the Montanists, Novatians, Donatists... Paulicians... adherents to apostolic doctrine and practice and link in the chain of Baptist Apostolic succession ... no one of them can be proved to have held Baptist views as to the nature and subject of baptism... We are not able to prove, it is true, that from the close of the apostolic age to the twelfth century a single congregation existed that was in every particular true to the apostolic norm." (Newman, History of the Baptist Churches in the United States, pp. 12-13.)

ALBIGENSES

"They arose in Southern France early in the eleventh century. They were first called Albigenses by Stephen Borbone, 1225." (Armitage, History of the Baptist, p. 278.)

"The sects began to appear about the year 1000... The earliest in Western Europe were known as Albigenses." (McGlothlin, The Course of Christian History, p. 80.)

"It appears... that they had a Pope who had come from far-off Bulgaria, and who carefully defined the bounds of their various Catharist bishopric." (Armitage, History of the Baptists, p. 286.)

DO YOU CALL THESE GOOD BAPTISTS?

"The Paulicians, Cathari, Albigenses, and in fact the modern Quakers, all cast infant baptism aside, but administered no baptism at all." (Armitage, Ibid., p. 283.)

"Though they were themselves unscriptural in some of

their doctrines..." (McGlothlin, The Course of Christian History, p. 80.)

PETROBRUSIANS

"Peter of Bruys began his career as a reformer in the year 1104." (Cramps, Baptist History, p. 98.)

"In the twelfth century in Western Switzerland and Eastern France (Some sprang up) known as Petrobrusians and Henricians." (W.J. McGlothlin, The Course of Christian History, p. 80.)

"In the Petrobrusians we find a sect of Baptists for which no apology is needed... He was a converted Priest... brought to the Saviour's feet by reading the Bible. There he saw the difference between the Christianity of his day and of that of the Apostles; and he resolved to devote his life to the restoration of Gospel Christianity, and began his work as early as A.D. 1104 ... In their enthusiasm the people burned their images and crucifixes, some Catholic places of worship were overturned, and many monks and priests were handled very severely... by terror and torture they are compelled to marry wives." (Armitage, History of the Baptists, pp. 284-287.)

ACCUSATION AGAINST THEM:

"...denying that little children under years of responsibility can be saved by the baptism of Christ. . . because, according to them, not another's faith, but personal faith, saves with baptism, the Lord saying, 'He who shall believe, and be baptized, shall be saved, but he that believeth not shall be condemned'... Peter assumes without evidence that the Petrobrusians believed that baptism was essential to salvation ... it is clear that the Petrobrusians were very decided Bible Baptists." (William Cathcart, The Baptist Encyclopedia, II, 912-914.)

"According to them, it is not another's but one's own faith which, together with baptism, saves, because the Lord

said, 'Whosoever believeth and is baptized shall be saved."
(Armitage, op. cit., p. 285.)
WERE THESE BAPTISTS?

WALDENSES

"Prof. Emile Comba has recently given us the best and only reliable history of the Waldenses translated by T.E. Comba, London, 1888. He gives up al! attempt to trace their history to Apostolic times, and finds their origin in Peter Waldo." (Hurst, Short History of the Christian Church, footnote, p. 153.)

"...originated about 1170 at Lyons in Southern France." (W.J. McGlothlin, The Course of Christian History, p. 80.)

"The ablest modern historians do not find them beyond the great reformer Waldo." (Thomas Armitage, History of the Baptists, p. 294.)

"At the time this extraordinary man (Waldo) began his evangelical career, it (Gospel truth, J.P. W.) was sunk in the grossest darkness and superstition. Waldo, at first, like other great reformers, had not the most distant idea of withdrawing himself from the communion of the Romish church." (David Benedict, History of the Baptists, p. 23.)

"The early Waldenses (1178 onward) were believers in transubstantiation, baptismal regeneration, and infant baptism." (A.H. Newman, History of the Baptist Churches in the United States, p. 15.)

WERE THESE GOOD BAPTISTS?

"Neither Waldo nor his followers had any thought of seceding from the Church. Like the Pietists of Germany in the last century, they hoped to produce reform within the Church. But their efforts soon met with fierce opposition. The Archbishop of Lyons issued a decree against them." (Hurst, Short History of the Christian Church, pp. 153-154.)

"If they opposed infant baptism it is unaccountable that

their literature, running through four centuries, gives no formal argument against it, and no accompanying demand for the baptism of believers only." (Thomas Armitage, History of the Baptists, p. 302.)

"On baptism the Waldenses were divided. There is reason to believe that some of them practiced infant baptism." (William Cathcart, The Baptist Encyclopedia, II, 1200-1201.)

"There are few of the baptists of the present day, it is to be hoped, who would blush to own an alliance with either of the old Waldensian preachers, or the heretical baptists referred to by this father of the Catholic church." (David Benedict, History of the Baptists, p. 28.)

"No one can make a study of the Waldenses and fail to see very rapidly that they held the two doctrines essential to a Baptist church... Baptists need feel no shame in claiming kin with them." (Roy Mason, The Church That Jesus Built, p. 135.)

"These Baptists descended from the Waldenses." (J.R. Graves, Trilemma, p. 121.)

"Indeed, in some cases, the Baptists evidently sprang from the Waldensians." (Thomas Armitage, History of the Baptists, p. 304.)

"They were apprehended, and brought before a council of the clergy at Oxford... Gerard, a man of learning, answered in their name, that they were Christians, and believed the doctrines of the apostles." (D.B. Ray, Baptist Church Succession, p. 371.)

"They called themselves Christians, believers and disciples, and claimed to be the followers of Christ and the apostles, and this is about all we know of their theological creed." (David Benedict, History of the Baptists, p. 59.)

They confessed that baptism without faith, is ineffectual to salvation." (David Benedict, Ibid., p. 75.)

ANABAPTISTS

"As to the origin of the Anabaptists, church historians differ." (Roy Alason, The Church That Jesus Built, p. 137.)

"Their very uncertainty, and their complete divergence of opinion about the matter is in itself a good argument for the thing they oppose." (Roy Mason, Ibid., p. 115.)

"An Anabaptist is one who baptized again for any reason." (Thomas Armitage, History of the Baptist, p. 283.)

"On November 13, 1644, the following law was promulgated: 'Forasmuch as experience hath plentifully proved that since the first arising of the Anabaptists, about a hundred years since, they have been the incendiaries of commonwealths and the infecters of persons in main matters of religion'." (A.H. Newman, History of the Baptist Churches in the United States, pp. 126-127.)

"Storch's party attempted to carry out their ideas of force, and proclaimed that they had a mission to establish the kingdom of Christ on earth... claiming a special inspiration of God to interpret Scriptures ... It may be remarked that while none of the Anabaptists were free from what we regard as errors, the great body of Swiss Anabaptists made a very close approach to our position... Fundamentally they were Baptists, but it required time for them to reach a complete development." (William Cathcart, The Baptist Encyclopedia, I, 26-28.)

"The fact is, the Munster Anabaptists were many of them sprinklers." (J.R. Graves, Trilemma, p. 125.)

"Anabaptists first appeared in England in the earlier portion of the sixteenth century ... In fact, few Anabaptists anywhere were immersionists." (W.H. Whitsitt, A Question in Baptist History, pp. 34, 35.)

"Some persons imagine that the Anabaptists of the times of the Reformation, and Baptists of our day are the same. But they are as different as possible... The English and Dutch Baptists do not consider the word as at all applicable to their sect." (Orchard, A Concise History of Foreign

Baptists, Introduction by J.R. Graves, p. 16.)

"The Baptists of today are the descendants of the Anabaptists who have, for so many centuries, witnessed for Christ, against the corruptions of Antichrist." J.R. Graves, Trilemma, p. 79.)

"In their uprising some outrages were committed; castles had been burned and plundered and ruthless oppressors had been slain. These deeds were now made the pretext for a retaliation whose cruelty has rarely been surpassed in history. It is computed by historians who have no motive to exaggerate, that fully a hundred thousand were killed before the fury of the princes and the knights was appeased." (H.C. Vedder, Short History of the Baptists, p. 173.)

"Munzer, and his associates, in the year 1525, put themselves at the head of a very numerous army, and declared war against all laws, governments, and magistrates of every kind, under the chimerical pretext that Christ himself was now to take the reins of all governments into his hands: but this seditious crowd was routed and dispersed by the elector of Saxony, and other Princes, and Munzer, their leader, put to death." (D.B. Ray, Baptist Church Succession, p. 92.)

CHAPTER 3
ORIGIN OF MODERN BAPTISTS

"FAITH PUBLICLY EXPRESSED, by a voluntary submission to his authority and doctrine in baptism. Wherever this conduct is evident, we claim the disciple as belonging to our communion and of primitive character." (Orchard, A Concise History of Foreign Baptists, Introduction, p. 14, by J.R. Graves.)

"To affirm that a man is a Baptist proves nothing more than that he rejects infant baptism and holds to believers baptism, by immersion." (David Benedict, History of All Denominations, p. 198.)

"A Baptist proper, in modern parlance, is one who rejects the baptism of babes under all circumstances, and who immerses none but those who personally confess Christ under any circumstances." (Thomas Armitage, History of the Baptists, p. 283.)

"I would engage to show that baptism as viewed and practiced by the Baptists, had its advocates in every century up to the Christian era. That the first FORTY-FOUR WRITERS after the apostles, now called orthodox, never once mentioned any other baptism than that for which we contend. That all the writers of the first and second centuries, inspired and uninspired, speak of a believer as the only subject, and of immersion as the only baptism. In the third century infant baptism was introduced, but only in certain cases... hosts in the sixteenth century have advocated the Baptist sentiment and practice... clouds of witnesses attest the fact, that before the Reformation from popery, and from the apostolic age to the present time, the sentiment of Baptists, and the practice of baptism, have had a continued chain of advocates, and public monuments of their existence in every century can be produced." (Alexander Campbell, Campbell-McCalla Debate, pp. 338-339.)

"The Baptists, as now distinguished from other Protestant parties, began since the Protestant Reformation... About the middle of the seventeenth century (1643) seven churches in London, and afterwards (July 7, 1689) about one hundred churches in England and Wales, met in London and fully set forth their faith and opinions in the form of a 'Confession,' of which I have the ninth American edition—Philadelphia, 1798—adopted by the Baptist Association met in Philadelphia, September 25, 1742. From this document and its history, we can give to the Baptist denomination a habitation and a name two hundred years old." (Alexander Campbell, Millennial Harbinger, New Series, V, No. 9, Sept. 1841). (This makes him say they are from 1641, J.P. W.)

"The history of Baptist churches cannot be carried, by the scientific method, farther back than the year 1611, when the first Anabaptist church consisting wholly of Englishmen was founded in Amsterdam by John Smyth, the Se-Baptist." (H.C. Vedder, Short History of the Baptists, Introduction, p. 4.)

"The first regularly organized Baptist church of which we possess any account, is dated from 1607, and was formed in London by a Mr. Smyth, who had been a clergyman in the church of England." (David Benedict, History of the Baptists, p. 304.)

"On arriving at Amsterdam, Smyth at first united with the 'ancient' English Separatist Church there, in charge of Johnson, with Ainsworth as teacher. At that time the Separatists of Amsterdam were in warm controversy on the true nature of a visible church... This led Smyth, Helwys, Morton and thirty-six others to form a new church which should practice believers baptism and reject infant baptism. Finding themselves unbaptized, they were in a strait... with the design of restoring this pattern, he baptized himself on his faith in Christ in 1608, then baptized Thomas Helwys with about forty others, and so formed a new church in Amsterdam." (Thomas Armitage, History of the Baptists, pp. 453-454.)

"There is less clear and decisive evidence of the practice of immersion amongst the English Baptists from 1600 to 1641 than might be desired, but the passage cited from Leonard Busher, and other proofs, render it certain that they did not first practice it in 1641. It is quite clear that some of them practiced affusion up to that time, while some immersed, but after that date affusion seems to have ceased amongst them and only immersion obtained. The case of John Smyth, who baptized himself in 1608, may be conceded to have been an affusion, and yet this is by no means certain, neither has his immersion been proved." (Thomas Armitage, Ibid., p. 439.)

"According to the unanimous testimony of contemporaries and his own apparent admission, Smyth first baptized himself, then Thomas Helwys, and afterward the rest of the company. It is almost certain that the rite was administered by affusion and not by immersion." (A.H. Newman, History of the Baptist Churches in the United States, p. 41.)

"That the name Baptist first came into use shortly after 1641, is another evidence of the fact in question... The name Baptist was in 1644 first claimed by our people. They have claimed it ever since." (William T Whitsitt, A Question in Baptist History, pp. 92-93.)

"The name 'Baptist' was not a self chosen one ... Following what they believed to be apostolic precept and example, they made baptism on a profession of faith a condition of church fellowship. This rejection of infant baptism and this insistence on believers baptism were so distinctive of these Christians that they were stigmatized as 'Anabaptists,' 'Catabaptists,' and sometimes as simply "Baptists";" that is to say, they were declared to be 're- baptizers,' 'perverters of baptism,' or, as unduly magnifying baptism and making it the occasion of schism, simply 'baptizers.' These party names they earnestly repudiated, preferring to call themselves Brethren, Christians, Disciples of Christ, Believers, etc." (A.H. Newman, History of the Baptist Churches in the United States, Introduction, p. 1.)

"MAKE CHRISTIANS BAPTISTS. We are to make men Christians by preaching salvation through faith in Christ to them, then we are to make those Christians Baptists by baptizing them according to his orders... While the command to make disciples takes the place of precedence in the Commission, the command to make Baptists is just as obligatory and binding upon us. Some censure Baptists, claiming that they put too great an emphasis upon baptism." (Roy Mason, The Church That Jesus Built, p. 164.)

"Every individual Baptist church is a church of God. No others are." (Roy Mason, Ibid., p. 53.)

"Only baptized believers or Baptists are members of the churches of Christ." (Roy Mason, Ibid., p. 57.)

"For more than five hundred years from the coming of Austin into England,... impenetrable clouds of darkness are spread over the whole history of this kingdom, so far as the baptists are concerned, and no glances can be had of any people who bore any resemblance of them, until after the middle of the 11th century." (David Benedict, History of the Baptist, p. 305.)

"From the second to the fourth century, we find a rapid departure from inspired truth, with many sects, and no churches exactly after the Apostolic order." (Thomas Armitage, History of the Baptists, p. 5.)

"THE FIFTH CENTURY... This age is marked by the total eclipse of true justifying faith and the simple method of Gospel salvation." (Thomas Armitage, Ibid., p. 211.)

"THIRD PERIOD-323 TO 600 A.D. (p. 39.) Paul and the other laborers of early days would not have recognized the churches of their planting." (W.J. McGlothlin, The Course of Christian History, p. 49.)

"FOURTH PERIOD-600 TO 1050... There is an air of decline and decay over the whole world." (W.J. McGlothlin, Ibid., p. 52.)

"Not until we reach the twelfth century do we encounter types of Christian life that we can with any confidence recognize as Baptists." (A.H. Newman, History of the Baptist Churches in the United States, p. 13.)

"The wire of the Atlantic cable is of peculiar formation, peculiarly insulated, and history informs us that several years ago it was laid down across the entire ocean, from Valentia, Ireland, to Newfoundland. I suppose there are persons who stoutly deny this as quite improbable, if not impossible, and assert that I am foolish to believe it, and even call upon me for proof of its continuity before they will believe. I satisfy them that the wire cable that I trace from Valentia to the ocean, and for a thousand miles along the plateau, where it drops beyond my line, is the same with that which I find upon the plateau, on this side of the deep soundings, and onward to the telegraph station at Newfoundland... Still, those persons refuse to believe unless I will trace the continuity of that wire for the hundreds of miles of those almost soundless depths." (J. R- Graves, Old Landmarkism: What Is it?, pp. 125-126.)

"SUCCESSION OF CHURCHES.—I shall not attempt to trace a continuous line of churches, as we can for a few centuries past in Europe and America. This is a kind of succession to which we have never laid claim; and, of course, we make no effort to prove it. We place no kind of reliance on this sort of testimony to establish the soundness of our faith or the validity of our administration. ' (David Benedict, History of the Baptists, p. 51.)

"The destitution of gospel privileges in Wales about 1641 was truly appalling." (A.H. Newman, History of the Baptist Churches in the United States, p. 163.)

"EIGHTH PERIOD-1648 TO 1789 ... (p. 149) Life was unspeakably gross and evangelical faith seemed to be dead." (W.J. McGlothlin, The Course of Christian History, p. 158.)

"The writer can easily remember when Baptist Associations were wont to close their sessions by celebrating the Lord's Supper, and this they did for years; but was it right because our fathers did it? Who will advocate this practice today, or what Association on this continent will presume to administer the Supper?... Fifty years ago our fathers were wont to advise the churches to send their licentiates to the Association to receive ordinations, and it was wont to select a Presbytery, and between them ordain the ministers. But who will advocate so unscriptural a procedure now? Twenty-five or thirty years ago, the overwhelming majority of our churches in the south would indorse a Campbellite, and alien immersion as valid." (J.R. Graves, Old Landmarkism: What is It? pp. 81-82.)

"Little perception is required to discover the fallacy of a visible apostolical succession in the ministry, but visible church succession is precisely as fallacious, and for exactly the same reason. The Catholic is right in his theory that these two must stand or fall together... And many who are not Catholics think that if they fail to unroll a continuous succession of regularly organized churches, they lose their genealogy by a break in the chain, and so fail to prove that they are legitimate apostolic churches. Such evidence cannot be traced by any church on earth, and would be utterly worthless if it could, because the real legitimacy of Christianity must be found in the New Testament, and no where else. . . The idea is the very life of Catholicism. ... A church established today upon the New Testament life and order, would be as truly a historical church from Christ, as the church planted by Paul at Ephesus. Robert Robinson has well said: 'Uninterrupted succession is a specious lure, a snare set by sophistry, into which all parties have fallen.'... this matter of visible church successions is originally connected with the idea of church infallibility, rather than likeness of Christ. The twin doctrines were born of the same parentage, and the one implies the other, for a visible succession must be pure in all its parts, that is, infallible;... Pure doctrine, as it is found uncorrupted in the word of God, is the only unbroken line of succession which can be traced in Christianity." (Thomas Armitage, History of the Baptists, pp. 1-3.)

"If either Thomas Campbell or his son (Alexander Campbell), or both acting in concert, organized a church of the right kind of material, and on the right faith and foundation, then they acted in harmony with the word of God, and no man has the least right to open his mouth in opposition; for a church thus constituted would be none other than a church of Christ." (J.H. Milburn, Origin of Campbellism, p. 10.)

"Others have been influenced to believe that we hold to 'apostolic succession'; others, that we hold that baptism is essential to salvation." (J.R. Graves, Old Landmarkism: What Is it? Preface, p. 13.)

Chapter 4
MODERN BAPTISTS HAVE CHANGED

Shouting how they have changed on: Foot-washing, Dry Christening, Music, Titles, Associations, Invisible Church, and other things.

"The Baptists, too, it must be admitted, are not precisely what they would have been, had there been no Reformation." (J.B. Jeter, Campbellism Examined, p. 368.)

"It is most likely that in the Apostolic age when there was but 'one Lord, one faith, and one baptism,' and no differing denominations existed, the baptism of a convert by that very act constituted him a member of the church, and at once endowed him with all the rights and privileges of full membership. In that sense, 'baptism was the door into the church.' Now, it is different." (Edward T. Hiscox, Standard Baptist Church Manual, p. 22.)

"Even Baptists sometimes forget that their tradition has not the force of law." (H.C. Vedder, The Dawn of Christianity, p. 65.)

"A good many Baptists are in great danger of forgetting that their guesses have not the authority of Scriptures."[1] (H.C. Vedder, Ibid., p. 83.)

"We have moved away from the ground of Scriptural authority in such matters to the modern ground of the evidence of religious experience." (H. Wheeler Robinson, Life and Faith of the Baptists, p. 52.)

"If one believes that the Bible is inspired and infallible, then to speak where it speaks and be silent where it is silent, is to be infallible. Baptists do not claim to do this." (Dr. Albert Garner, tract "A Few Aspirins for Campbellites, pp. 14, 15.)

FOOT WASHING

"THE WASHING OF FEET. From time immemorial this oriental custom, so often referred to in the history of the early Christians, has been observed by small groups of Baptists, in a religious manner, in different parts of the country... with our people it has generally been discontinued." (David Benedict, Fifty Years Among Baptists, pp. 121-122.)

HAD ELDERS

"John Leland, in his Virginia Chronicle, in 1790, informs us that the DRY CHRISTENING ceremony prevailed to some extent in the Old Dominion at that time. This unusual rite among Baptists, which long since went out of use, was founded on the incident of parents bringing little children to Christ to bless them, and was thus performed: as soon as circumstances would permit, after the birth of a child, the mother carried it to meeting, when the minister either took it in his arms, or laid his hands on it, thanked God for his mercy, and invoked a blessing on the little one, in a public manner... called it a DRY CHRISTENING... They also held to RULING ELDERS, ELDERISSES, DEACONESSES, AND WEEKLY COMMUNION." (David Benedict, Ibid., pp. 122- 123.)

"Among those who seceded with Spilbury in 1633, and who were immersed in 1641, was Mark Iaikar, who was afterwards to occupy the position of ruling elder and to be a leading worker in John Clark's church at New Port." (A. LI. Newman, History of the Baptist Churches in the United States, p. 50.)

"Jeremiah Kirtley... united with Bulletsburg church, and was soon afterwards ordained an Elder in that body, a nominal office in some Baptist churches of that day, which, as the government of those churches then, as now, was purely democratic, seems to have been an officer without an office. It was practically a mere title of respect." (J.H. Spencer, A History of the Kentucky Baptists, p. 299.)

"This was an office distinct from that of a preacher, in some of the Baptist churches of that period." (J.H. Spencer, Ibid., p. 294.)

"It may be interesting to note that this (Newport) church was one of the first to introduce instrumental music. The instrument was a bass viol and caused considerable commotion. This occurred early in the nineteenth century." (A.H. Newman, History of the Baptist Churches in the United States, p. 255.)

INSTRUMENTAL MUSIC

"In my earliest intercourse among this people, congregational singing generally prevailed among them... THE INTRODUCTION OF THE ORGAN AMONG THE BAPTISTS. This instrument, which from time immemorial has been associated with cathedral pomp and prelatical power, and has always been the peculiar favorite of great national churches, at length found its way into Baptist sanctuaries, and the first one ever employed by the denomination in this country, and probably in any other, might have been seen standing in the singing gallery of the Old Baptist meeting house in Pawtucket, about forty years ago, where I then officiated as pastor (1840)... Staunch old Baptists in former times would as soon tolerated the Pope of Rome in their pulpits as an organ in their galleries, and yet the instrument has gradually found its way among them... How far this modern organ fever will extend among our people, and whether it will on the whole work a RE-formation or DE-formation in their singing service, time will more fully develop." (David Benedict, Fifty Years Among Baptists, pp. 204-207.)

REVEREND

"The term REVEREND, now in such common use

among our people and all other parties, was generally very offensive to Baptists of the old school." (David Benedict, Ibid, p. 208.)

"They regarded the assumption of the title of 'Doctor of Divinity' as 'blasphemy.' What will our modern D.D.s think of this?" (D.B. Ray, Baptist Church Succession, p. 426.)

WEEKLY COMMUNION

"The Mennonites celebrated the Supper once or twice a year and were opposed to the weekly celebration; the English (Baptists) found great comfort in the weekly celebration and pleaded earnestly to be tolerated in this practice." (A.H. Newman, History of the Baptist Church in the United States, p. 47.)

1786. "They had ceased to lay stress on love- feasts, laying on of hands, feet-washing, the anointing of the sick, the kiss of charity, the ceremonial devotion of children, and weekly communion." (A.H. Newman, Ibid., p. 302.)

1854. "There is no objection to weekly communion, ... it is admitted that among the early churches, it is highly probable, that it did generally, if it did not universally prevail. I do not perceive any solid objection against returning to the practice." (J.B. Jeter, Campbellism Examined, p. 288.)

ASSOCIATIONS AND CONVENTIONS

"In New Testament times there were no Mission Societies such as Boards, Conventions, Associations and Missionary Committees. The churches were the medium through which the Holy Spirit worked to send the gospel out to the world." (L.S. Ballard in his paper. 1/1/48.)

"In the year 1650, the baptist churches began to form themselves into associations." (David Benedict, History of the Baptists, p. 304.)

"For nearly seventy years the Baptists of America had

no associations." (Throgmorton, Potter- Throgmorton Debate, p. 106.)

"If I should ask for the word 'association,' Brother Potter could not show it in all the New Testament as applied to such a body. (Throgmorton, Ibid., p. 14.)

"A missionary convention is somewhat like an association." (Ibid., p. 15.)

"When churches meet together in associations and conventions they come together in only a cooperative, voluntary way." (Roy Mason, The Church That Jesus Built, p. 98.)

"In 1926, certain changes were noted: .... A new body was organized, under the name Independent Baptist Church of America; and a new denomination came out of the Southern Baptist Convention, called the American Baptist Association." (U.S. Department of Commerce, Bureau of Census, Religious Bodies, Vol.2, p.85.)

Dr. J.E. Cobb says, "...the Government's Report on Religious Bodies in the United States of America. This gives, usually, the date of origin, the principle tenets of doctrine, and the number of members and churches, and is about as authoritative source as one could obtain." (J.E. Cobb, New Church Manual, p. 214.)

"AMERICAN B.T. C. ASSEMBLY IS FORMED." (American Baptist Paper, ed. Dr. D.N. Jackson, September 13, 1941.)

"I started the B.T. C. work among our people and in December, 1918 I wrote the first B.T. C. quarterly ever published among us." (Ibid., March 12, 1947.)

A BIG UNIVERSAL CHURCH

"The Catholick or universal Church, which (with respect to internal work of the Spirit, and truth of grace) may be called invisible, consists of the whole number of the Elect, that has been, are, or shall be gathered into one, under Christ the head thereof; and is the spouse, the body, the fullness of him that filleth all in all." (W.J. McGlothlin, Baptist Concessions of Faith, p. 264).

"There is one holy catholick church, consisting of, or made up of the whole number of the elect, that have been, are, or shall be gathered, in one body under Christ, the only head thereof." (Ibid., p. 145.)

"In the New Testament, however, the term ekklesia, (generally translated church) in its application to the followers of Christ, refers either to a particular congregation of saints, or to the redeemed in the aggregate." (J.M. Pendleton, Three Reasons Why I Am A Baptist, pp. 34-35.)

"Baptists must,... look alone among themselves for visible churches of Christ." (J.M. Pendleton, Pillars of Orthodoxy, p. 271.)

"Neither Pedobaptists nor Quakers have baptism among them, and 'where there is no baptism there are no visible churches.'" (Ibid., p. 276.)

"Pedobaptist ministers are not in the visible kingdom of Christ. How then can they induct others into it by baptism?" (Ibid., p. 280.)

"We both believe that baptism is a prerequisite to membership in a visible church of Christ." (Ibid., p. 298.)

"A visible church without baptism. How can this be?... The day has been when Baptists had never heard or thought of a visible church without baptism—nor had Pedobaptists. The times are now changed, and Baptists may be found who are determined to have Pedobaptists in the visible churches of Christ without baptism—a thing that Pedobaptists themselves consider impossible." (Ibid., p. 305.)

"Says Dr. E. '(believers) may be saved, or belong to the church universal.' Yes, but the discussion is not about the 'church universal,' but about visible churches of Christ. There is no universal visible church; and if the universal invisible church, composed of all the saved, has what Dr. E. calls 'form,' it is impossible to know what it is. We have no idea of 'form' apart from visibility." (Ibid., p. 304.)

"My position is that, according to the gospel, authority to preach must, under God, emanate from a visible church of Christ. Hence members of a visible church alone are eligible to the work of the ministry." (Ibid., p. 310.)

"...excommunication, by which they were placed outside of the visible kingdom of God, and, so to speak, replaced in the realm of Satan... The general representation of Scripture, that outside the visible kingdom of God on earth is the kingdom of Satan, is here probably the underlying conception. ' (Alvah H. Hovey, American Commentary, Vol. 6, 28.)

(Today, Baptist debaters all, so far as I know, deny such a thing as an invisible, or universal church. They have changed on this matter.)

JOHN'S BAPTISM

They once taught John's baptism was different to the baptism introduced by our Lord, but today they teach that it is the same.

"John's baptism was unto repentance and faith in him who was to come. Jesus baptized (or his disciples did) into himself, as the Messiah who had come." (Hiscox, The New Directory for Baptist Churches, p. 121.)

"In our opinion, the differences between the baptism of John and that of the apostles, after the ascension of Jesus, were circumstantial, and not fundamental." (J.B. Jeter, Baptist Principles Reset, p, 34.)

"It has been made a question respecting the baptism of John, whether it was the same as the ordinance instituted by Christ (Matt. 28:19) ... we are decidedly of the opinion that it was not the same, but merely an introductory rite, designed to prepare the way for the gospel dispensation; and in this we agree, not only with the ancient church, but with the most respectable writers, Baptist and Pedobaptists, of the present day... This baptism took place under the JEWISH DISPENSATION. The Jewish dispensation continued in force till the ' death of Christ... Our Saviour lived under the old dispensation, and was a strict observer of the institution of Moses;... Christian baptism originated in the express command of Christ: 'Go ye and teach all nations, baptizing them in the name of the Father, and of the Son, and of the Holy Ghost.' No such origin can be claimed for the baptism of John, who baptized for some time BEFORE HE KNEW CHRIST. John 1:31. He ascribes his commission to the FATHER, John 1.33. The baptism of John was EVIDENTLY a preparatory ordinance... The baptism of John, unlike Christian baptism, was not administered in the name of the Father, the Son, and the Holy Ghost... Indeed, John did not baptize in the name of Christ, or in any other name; but merely directed those who came to his baptism to 'believe on him who should come after him,' Acts 19:4." (J. Newton Brown, Baptist, Encyclopedia of Religious Knowledge, pp. 177-178.)

"Now the faith which John preached before Christ came, was not the proper faith to be preached after he came; since he required them to believe that Christ was YET TO COME, and no one but John was authorized to administer his baptism." (J.R. Graves, Old Landmarkism: What Is It?, p. 66.)

THEY ONCE SAID ANY COULD DO THE BAPTIZING

"Ordained ministers of God's word are the proper administrators of the ordinances. There is, indeed, for this no positive divine precept, but it is the natural order... The validity of an ordinance, however, does not depend on the administrator, bur on the character of the recipient... Hence, the validity of baptism in the case of those immersed on a personal profession of faith is to be recognized, even when administered by men not themselves baptized." (H. Harvey, The Church, p. 107.)

"In the Broadmead Church, Thomas Jennings, who appears to have been an ordained minister, was the 'usual administrator' of baptism; but any preacher, ordained or not, might baptize." (Cramp, Baptist History, p. 386.)

"But he (Roger Williams) was manifestly in error in making the validity of Christian ordinances to depend upon any ceremonial or personal qualification of the administrator." (Newman, History of the Baptist Churches in the United States, p. 83.)

"The baptism followed immediately on the eunuch's profession of faith. So far as the record shows, it lacked the authority of any church or ecclesiastic, and was administered by one who is not known to have received ordination as a minister... only by authority of a church, was not uniform in New Testament times, especially in the earlier years of the church. Even Baptists sometimes forget that their tradition has not the force of law." (H.C. Vedder, The Dawn of Christianity, p. 64.)

MARK 16:16

THEY ONCE USED MARK 16:16 FLUENTLY, BUT SOME HAVE QUIT AND CONSIDER IT SPURIOUS. Newman's, History of the Baptist Churches, shows that it was used as good scripture among Baptists in their early days, (pp. 14 and 16) as well as most old works of Baptists. On this they have also changed.

"Mr. Borden contends that baptism precedes salvation. Where did he find that? Only in Mark 16:16. But now, ladies and gentlemen, Mark 16:16, according to the best scholars, writers and translators of the Bible, is not inspired." (Dr. L.S. Ballard, Borden-Ballard Debate, p. 128.)

G.E. Jones denies it in his book, "Tribe of Ishmael," p. 22.

Dr. J.E. Cobb and Dr. D.N. Jackson never refer to it in their books, even on such subjects as baptism or the great commission. If you search their books you will see that this is true.

Ben M. Bogard says, in the "Hardeman-Bogard Debate," page 273, "I HAVE NEVER YET SAID THAT MARK 16:16 WAS A PART OF THE WORD OF GOD." (His caps, J.P. W.) Yet, in the first edition of Mr. Bogard's, "Baptist Way-Book, p. 41, he says, "THE WAY OF MISSION WORK IN HISTORY. The Apostolic Baptists were Missionary Baptists. This is abundantly proved by the Master's commanding the church to 'go into all the world and preach the gospel to every creature.'" In a later edition of this same book, Mr. Bogard says, "THE WAY OF MISSION WORK IN HISTORY. The Apostolic Baptists were Missionary Baptists. This is abundantly proved by the Master's commanding the church to go 'teach all nations, baptizing them.'" (page 42.) (The first quotation is Mk. 16:15. The last is Mt. 28:19, J.P. W.)

NOW THEY SAY THE GREAT COMMISSION WAS GIVEN TO THE CHURCH, BUT THEY TAUGHT IT DIFFERENTLY

"It was given to the church as such for the reason that Jesus promised to be with the church until the end." (D.N. Jackson, Ten Reasons Why I Am Baptist, p. 20.)

"The church at Jerusalem, which received the commission from Christ ..." (Dr. J.E. Cobb, New Church Manual, p. 28.)

OTHER CHURCHES ARE not made by Jesus. "He is not responsible for their existence, and they are not responsible for the carrying out of the Commission which he gave centuries before they came into being. But Baptists ARE responsible, because it was to a Baptist church that the Lord Jesus gave his Commission." (Roy Mason, The Church That Jesus Built, p. 161.)

"This Commission was given to Baptists, for everyone present was a Baptist. It is a very definite ' command to make men Christians by preaching the gospel to them, and

then to make them Baptists by giving them Baptist baptism." (Roy Mason, Ibid.,
p. 162.)

EARLIER VIEWS OF THE BAPTISTS.

"His commission (was) to the apostles, and to all succeeding ministers." (J. Newton Brown, Baptist, Encyclopedia of Religious Knowledge, p. 181.)

"In giving the 'Great Commission' to the Apostles, the risen Lord commanded...." (J.W. Wilmarth, Baptism and Remission, Baptist Quarterly, July 1877, p. 309.)

"4. THE COMMISSION GIVEN BY THE SAVIOUR TO HIS APOSTLES JUST BEFORE HIS ASCENSION TO HEAVEN, FURNISHES NO PLEA FOR INFANT BAPTISM." (J.M. Pendleton, Three Reasons Why I Am A Baptist, p. 10.)

"I affirm that the commission of Christ to the apostles requiring them to baptize disciples, believers, prohibits, in effect, the baptism of all others." (Ibid., p. 13.)

"The commission of Christ to his apostles requires the baptism of believers." (Ibid., p. 16.) Do you see these changes?

THEY ONCE ACCEPTED BAPTISM FROM OTHER CHURCHES, EVEN THE DENOMINATIONS

In 1791 "The case of James Hutchinson, whose immersion by a Methodist minister had been accepted by the Georgia Baptists but repudiated by the Baptists of Virginia, caused considerable embarrassment, and it was the opinion of the Georgia Baptist leaders that a serious mistake had been made in the matter." (A.H. Newman, History of the Baptist Churches in the United States, pp. 330-331.)

"It is simply idle to reject Bunyan's immersion by Gifford because his name does not appear on the Church record as an immersed member. For the same reason the immersion of Hanserd Knollys, John Clarke and Obediah Holmes may be rejected." (Thomas Armitage, History of the Baptists, p. 516.)

"J.M. Weaver was the last preacher licensed in Bloomfield church. In his youth Mr. Weaver joined the Methodist church and was immersed, upon a profession of his faith, by a Methodist preacher. He was received into Bloomfield church 'on his Methodist baptism,' and licensed to preach June 12, 1852... After some years he accepted a call to the pastorate of Chestnut Street (Baptist J.P.) church, in Louisville, of which he has been the able, beloved and successful pastor for about a dozen years. The irregularity of his baptism continued to be a subject of much discussion and no little dissatisfaction among churches, till the 5 th of July, 1879, when he was regularly baptized by Elder James P. Boyce." (J.H. Spencer, A History of the Kentucky Baptists, p. 230.)

CONCERNING THE ABOVE CASE: "Dr. Boyce said to Dr. Weaver: Why, I will baptize you and make it alright.' So one morning (our remembrance is that it was the Fourth of July) Dr. Boyce and Dr. Weaver were walking toward the Chestnut Street Church, when Dr. Boyce said: 'I will baptize you just now.' So the two went into the church, opened the baptistry, and Dr. Boyce baptized Dr. Weaver, though he was not himself a pastor and no vote of the church had been had. For a time the lack of church authority was kept secret; but it got out, and then came the laugh.... Dr. Boyce said ... 'I baptized Dr. Weaver on my own authority as a minister of the gospel'; and he was told that he undoubtedly had the right... Now, will our esteemed contemporaries be kind enough to tell us whether Dr. Weaver's baptism was valid, or must he be baptized again by authority of the church?" (Joe S. Warlick, Baptist Blunders, p. 36, quoted from Baptist paper "Journal & Messenger.")

A Handbook of Historical Briefs

"Twenty-five or thirty years ago, the overwhelming majority of our churches in the South would indorse a Campbellite, and alien immersion as valid." (J.R. Graves, Old Landmarkism: What Is It? p. 82.)

CHAPTER 5
BAPTISTS IN AMERICA

PROVIDENCE CHURCH

"In England the Arminians, but in America the Calvinistic Baptists were the earlier party. Roger Williams ... First church of Providence, the earliest Baptist church in America. At that date there was no Calvinistic Baptist Confession in existence. The church drew up none, and has continued to this day without any statement of doctrine...." (W.J. McGlothlin, Baptist Confessions of Faith, p. 293.)

"In 1639, he (Roger Williams) was baptized by Ezekiel Holliman, a layman who was appointed by the little company for the purpose. Then he (Williams) baptized the rest of the company, and thus laid the foundation for the first Baptist church in Providence, and on the American continent." (David Benedict, History of the Baptists, pp. 441-442.)

"Sometime about March 1639, therefore, Williams was baptized by Ezekiel Holliman, who had been a member of his church at Salem; and thereupon Williams baptized ten others, and the first Baptist church on American soil was formed." (H.C. Vedder, Short History of the Baptists, p. 291.)

"To Roger Williams belongs the distinction of being the first in America to introduce believers baptism and to organize a church on Baptist principles." (A.H. Newman, History of the Baptist Churches in the United States, p. 59.)

"This was the first Baptist church in America, although there is no evidence to show that they were immersed." (Frank Grenville Beardsley, Christianity in America, p. 20.)

"It appears that Mr. Williams did not mean to organize a Baptist church. He only meant to organize a church as near the Scriptures as possible." (Dr. D.N. Jackson, American Baptist Paper, July 10, 1943.)

(It appears to me that Dr. Jackson is here acknowledging that the Baptist church is not like the Scriptural church, because Williams didn't want to organize a Baptist church, BUT ONE LIKE THE SCRIPTURES. Agreed, and thanks, Doctor. J.P. W.)

"Roger Williams was the real founder of the Baptist church in America." (Hurst, Short History of the Christian Church, p. 516.)

"Roger Williams, a distinguished and honored name, was identified with the rise of the denomination in America. He has been called their founder, because he originated the first church, and was intimately connected with their early history." (Hiscox, The New Directory for Baptist Churches, p. 512.)

"In the month of March, 1639, Mr. Williams, whose tendency to Baptist views had long been apparent, was publicly immersed... Thus was founded what is commonly regarded as the oldest Baptist church in America." (William Cathcart, The Baptist Encyclopedia, II, 1252.)

"Having embraced the principles of the Baptists, and submitted to baptism, Mr. Williams founded the first Baptist church in Providence, in 1638." (J. Newton Brown, Encyclopedia of Religious Knowledge, p. 1170.)

"Williams did not remain in communion with , the church long, but it lived and still exists as the first Baptist church of Providence." (W.J. McGlothlin, The Course of Christian History, pp. 138-139.)

NEW PORT CHURCH

"If we accept the view, which is generally held, that the Providence church is the older, let it be remembered that Dr. Clark's long ministry gives to the New Port church a unique distinction." (Wilbur Nelson, The Hero of Aquidneck—A Life of John Clark, pp. 73-74.)

"Though second to the Providence church in point of date." (A.H. Newman, History of the Baptist Churches in the United States, p. 96.)

IN 1640—"It seems a safe conclusion that at this time this was not a Baptist church." (H.C. Vedder, Short History of the Baptists, p. 294.)

"A church was formed in 1641, of which Clark was pastor, probably another Congregational church, for we have no sign that even then he held Baptist views of the ordinances." (Thomas Armitage, History of the Baptists, pp. 670-671.)

"These things taken together lead to the highly probable conclusion, that Clark became a Baptist somewhere between 1640 and 1644, but we have no record of the time of his baptism, or that of his church... It is said to have been a daughter of Providence church, which was constituted about six years before." (Ibid., p. 671.)

"Dr. John Clarke and others organized the first Baptist church in America." (Dr. D.N. Jackson, Ten Reasons Why I Am A Baptist, p. 14.)

"In a manuscript said to be in the possession of the Backus Historical Society, Mr. Comer repeated the statement that 'the church was first gathered by Mr. Clark about 1644.'" (Henry Burrage, History of the New England Baptists, p. 25.)

OFFICERS

"The (Newport) church was furnished with a board of elders; among the earliest were Joseph Torrey, Obadiah Holmes, Mark Lucar, and John Crandall." (William Cathcart, The Baptist Encyclopedia, II, 841.)

"Their (Clark et al) first settlement was at the north end of the island, at what is now Portsmouth. ... At one time, it was supposed that this was' a religious compact, because they appointed 'three elders,' January 2, 1639." (Thomas Armitage, History of the Baptists, pp. 669-670.)

"It is recorded that in 1710 and the year following, several able men, ministers and elders,... came over from South Wales and the west of England,... and some that had been ruling elders in the churches where they came from." (A. H. Newman, History of the Baptist Churches in the United States, p. 212.)

"During the early history of the Providence church it appears that plurality of elders prevailed." (Ibid., p. 85.)

"RULING ELDERS were nominal officers in many of our earlier churches. ... In a Baptist church the term is a misnomer... There being no place in Baptist church polity, for the office of ruling elders, the churches were constantly perplexed to know what to do with it." (J.H. Spencer, A History of the Kentucky Baptists, p. 485.)

"These officers are no where mentioned as being alone or single, but always as being many in every congregation.... This office, more than once, is described as being distinct from that of preaching, not only in Rom. 12, where he that ruleth is expressly distinguished from him that exhorteth or teacheth, but also in that passage, 1 Tim. 5:17." (J. Newton Brown, Encyclopedia of Religious Knowledge, p. 494.)

"It was customary in the early stages of the movement of the churches to appoint 'ruling elders,'... From 1819 onward there was a growing sentiment against this office." (A.H. Newman, History of the Baptist Churches in the United States, pp. 497-498.)

"In Scotland .... (Baptist) church organizations are purely congregational, with a plurality of elders in some churches. They observe the Supper Weekly." (Thomas Armitage. History of the Baptists, p. 577.)

"In 1795, ... he (Robert Hodgen) united with Severns Valley church, (Baptist) ... he was also an elder in that church." (J.H. Spencer, A History of the Kentucky Baptists, p. 242.)

"After taking a year to study the subject, Elkhorn Association disposed of the matter in 1790, as follows: 'QUERRY FROM COOPERS RUN— Whether the office of elders, distinct from that of minister, be a gospel institution or not? ANSWER: It is the opinion of the Association that it is a gospel institution." (Ibid., p. 485.)

LORD'S SUPPER

"About the year 1755, Robert Sandeman developed and sustained their views and engaged in a spirited controversy with Hervey... He advocated the weekly observance of the Lord's Supper;... plurality of elders in a church." (Richardson, Memoirs of Campbell, I, 70.)

"James Alexander Haldane also visited Rich-Hill, and preached during Mr. Campbell's residence there." (Ibid., I, 60.)

"James Haldane ... at length settled as the pastor of the large congregation at Leith Walk, Edinburg." (Hurst, Short History of the Christian Church, p. 379.)

"From the church of Christ worshipping at Leith Walk, Edinburg... This was James A. Haldanes famous congregation." (M.M. Davis, How the Disciples Began and Grew, p. 25.)

LOYD GEORGE SAID, "A very large part of economics and social principles I am pressing on the English people I obtained from reading the writings of Alexander Campbell." (Ibid., p. 42.)

THESE EARLY AMERICAN BAPTISTS ALSO OBSERVED THE SUPPER EACH LORD'S DAY.

"The Christians were at first greatly attached to the temple in Jerusalem... ORDER OF SERVICE... Singing of psalms and hymns was an important part of the service,... the music was by the whole congregation.... The concluding part of the service was the Lord's Supper." (Hurst, Short History of the Christian Church, p. 20.)

"There was singing and prayer,... The services often if

not usually took place at night, on the first day of the week called the 'Lord's day' because of the resurrection and appearance of our Lord on that day... The Lord's Supper was celebrated with bread and wine as the memorial of the Lord's death." (W.J. McGlothlin, The Course of Christian History, p. 18.)

"John Glass,... who abandoned the Establishment about the year 1728, and adopted Independent views, which he derived mainly from the works of John Owen, ... he practiced breaking bread weekly." (Richardson, Memoirs of Campbell, I, 70.)

"Dale was gradually led to reject creeds and other human compositions,... and to appeal to the Scriptures alone.... "(In footnote)"... When he became an Independent, and adopted weekly communion, ... In 1769 one of his friends built a meeting house, and, a church was organized by the election of a number of elders." (Ibid., I, 185.)

UNITY

"People not acquainted with the subject are surprised to find in the books of Glass and Sandeman, the Haldanes and Dr. Kirk, ideas, arguments, doctrines, and even phrases, that our reformation has made familiar to the world." (J.J. Haley, Makers and Molders of the Reformation Movement, p. 18.)

"The Haldanes regarded the writings of Glass and Sandeman as exhibiting, here and there, noble views of the freeness of the gospel and the simplicity of faith." (Richardson, Memoirs of Campbell, I, 177.)

"While yet in Scotland, the Campbell's, and especially Thomas (for Alexander was not yet out of his teens), were impressed with the necessity and desirability of discussing Christian union by an appeal to the word of God, and this necessity and desirability was impressed upon his mind by the Haldaneon Reformation." (John F. Rowe, Reformation Movement, p. 128.)

"It will be seen, further, that the positions taken by the Christian Association at this period were almost identical with those held by the churches established by the Haldanes." (Richardson, Memoirs of Campbell, I, 349.)

"The antecedents of Thomas and Alexander Campbell, including their connection with Scottish sects, and the manifest influence of Sandemanianism on their modes of religious thought." (A.H. Newman, History of the Baptist Churches in the United States, p. 488.)

"In August, 1809, he (Thomas Campbell) organized his followers into the 'Christian Association of Washington' (County), Pennsylvania... deploring human creeds and systems... holding that they should follow the example of the New Testament church." (Frank G. Beardsley, Christianity in America, p. 145.)

"Thomas Campbell sowed the germ thought of the current Reformation in the terse saying: 'Where the Scriptures speak we speak, and where the Scriptures are silent, we are silent.'... The

Reformation movement is dated from the time the above words were spoken." (D.N. Jackson, "Origin of the Campbellite Church," article in the "American Baptist" Sept. 26, 1942.)

"As late as 1831 Thomas Campbell was received into many Baptist pulpits and heard by Semple and Broadus during a trip to Virginia." (Errett Gates and Eri B. Hulbert, The Early Relations and Separation of Baptists and Disciples, 102.)

BAPTISM OF THE CAMPBELLS AND OTHERS

"Thomas and Alexander, his son, with five others of the family rejected infant baptism, and on June 12, 1812, were immersed on profession of their faith in Christ, in Buffalo Creek, by Elder Luce, and were received into the fellowship of the Brush Run Baptist Church." (Thomas Armitage, History of the Baptists, p. 735.)

"He used these memorable words to Loos, the Baptist minister, who baptized him: 'I have set out to follow the apostles of Christ, and their Master, and I will be baptized only into the primitive Christian faith." (Hurst, Short History of the Christian Churches, pp. 558-559.)

"I had no idea of uniting with the Baptists, more than with the Moravians or the mere Independent." (Richardson, Memoirs of Campbell, I, 438.)

"In 1812, he was immersed by Elder Luce, a Baptist minister, without the action or authority of any Baptist church, and contrary to invariable and recognized law and usages of Baptist churches." (J.R. Graves, Trilemma, p. 191.)

"He (Alexander Campbell) brought with him the Reformation in embryo. Before he left the father-land, his faith 'in creeds and confessions of human device' was considerably shaken." (J.B. Jeter, Campbellism Examined, pp. 14-15.)

"I have enjoyed very fair opportunities of forming correct opinions of Mr. Campbell's system. I first saw him in the year 1825. Since that time, I have been a careful observer of his course. I have watched the gradual development of his principles, and marked their influence on the churches." (Ibid., Intro, p. xi.)

"The Baptist Society invited Mr. Campbell to make a translation of the book of Acts for their version, which he did." (A.T. DeGroot, Three Fourths of a Loaf, p. 3. Reprinted from "The Chronicle, a Baptist Historical Quarterly, April 1, 1948.)

"The title of his (Campbells) monthly periodical—'The Christian Baptist'—might seem to identify him with the Baptist denomination; but the appearance was illusory." (J.B. Jeter, Campbellism Examined, p. 24.) This paper was started in 1823, and he was baptized by Luce in 1812.

"No intelligent Christian can object to the end which Mr. Campbell proposed to accomplish. The union of all true Christians on the Apostolic foundation, is an object most devoutly to be wished. All good men pray for it." (Ibid.., p. 22.)

"The Baptists, too, it must be admitted, are not precisely what they would have been, had there been no Reformation." (Jeter, Ibid., p. 368.)

"The Reformers belong to the Baptist family, though, in our view, they are an erring branch of it." (Ibid., p. 359.)

"About this time (1855) there was published a book... entitled 'Campbellism Examined,' by Elder J.B. Jeter, of Richmond, Virginia. In this work the author, a Baptist minister of distinction, proposed to give a 'faithful delineation' of 'Campbellism,' a term by which he was pleased to designate the Reformation urged by Mr. Campbell... This work was therefore regarded by Mr. Campbell ... as doing him great injustice, and he proposed to Elder Jeter a discussion of the points involved, to be published in the 'Religious Herald,' so that his defense might be given to the Baptist community. This, however, Mr. Jeter declined." (Richardson, Memoirs of Campbell, II, 612, 613.)

Chapter 6
Baptists in America

Where and when as well as how, the church of Christ was connected with this history.

"The conversion of a man who was to be the Apostle of the Virginia Baptists. This was Col. Samuel Harris." (A.H. Newman, History of the Baptist Churches in the United States, p. 295.)

"As early as 1695, and a number of years before we have any direct historical account of any Baptists in Virginia, there were many individual Baptists, scattered along the eastern coast of North Carolina, supposed to have been driven out of Virginia, by the intolerant ecclesiastical laws of that colony... By the year 1752, sixteen churches had been gathered ... so zealous were they for baptism (as some of them expected salvation by it) that one of their preachers confessed, if he could get any willing to be baptized, and it was in the night, that he would baptize them by fire-light, for fear they should get out of the notion of it before the next morning... their doctrine and practice seems to have been substantially the same that are now held by the Campbellites." (J.H. Spencer, History of the Kentucky Baptists, pp. 97-98.)

"If either Thomas Campbell or his son, or both acting in concert, organized a church of the right kind of material, and on the right faith and foundation, then they acted in harmony with the word of God, and no man has the least right to open his mouth in opposition; for a church thus constituted would be none other than a church of Christ." (J.H. Milburn, Origin of Campbellism, p. 10.)

1792—"James O'Kelley, a Methodist presiding elder of Virginia, came into conflict with Bishop Asbury ... he withdrew from the denomination and organized a new party under the name 'Republican Methodist.' A few years later this designation was repudiated in favor of the name 'Christian,' and the Bible was declared to be the sole and sufficient authority in faith and practice." (A.H. Newman, History of the Baptist Churches in the United States, p. 502.)

"James O'Kelley, of North Carolina, and some other preachers of that state, and of Virginia, with a number of members, pleaded for a congregational system, and that the New Testament should be the only creed and discipline... these reformers were unable to accomplish their wishes and finally seceded at Manakin Town, North Carolina, December 25, 1793." (J.H. Milburn, Origin of Campbellism, p. 64.)

"Elias Smith was an ordained Baptist preacher in New England; he first gave up Calvinism and began to find the truth on matters of sin and redemption. He was joined in his efforts by another Baptist preacher whose name was Abner Jones. Smith and Jones together organized a 'Christian Church' at Portsmouth, New Hampshire, and withdrew from the fellowship of the Baptists." (G.C. Brewer, Foundation Facts, p. 18.)

"A physician of Hartland, Vermont, Abner Jones, then a member of the Baptist church, becoming dissatisfied with sectarian names and creeds, began to urge that all these should be abolished... In September, 1800, he succeeded by persevering zeal in establishing a church of twenty-five members at Lyndon, Vermont, and subsequently one in Bradford, and one in Pierpont, in March 1803." (J.H. Milburn, Origin of Campbellism, p. 65.)

"In 1800 Abner Jones, a Baptist of Vermont, became greatly disturbed 'in regard to sectarian names and human creeds,' and gathered a Christian church at Lyndon, Vt... within a short time the party had organizations in most or all of the New England states, New York, New Jersey, and Pennsylvania." (A.H. Newman, History of the Baptist Churches in the United States, pp. 501, 502.)

A Handbook of Historical Briefs

"In 1801 five Presbyterian ministers of Kentucky and Ohio,... not only repudiated the Calvinistic Presbyterian creed, but they insisted that the Bible alone is a sufficient standard of" faith and practice, declaring man-made creeds to be useless and pernicious... the name 'Christian' (was) adopted as the only proper designation of a body of believers. (Ibid., p. 501.)

"Barton W. Stone, who at his ordination (as Presbyterian preacher) stated that he received the Westminster Confession only so far as it was consistent with the word of God,... Having discarded all man-made creeds and confessions, and taking the Bible alone as the rule of faith and practice." (Frank G. Beardsley, Christianity in America, p. 103.)

"The reformed Baptists (Campbell and his brethren were called by that name) have received the doctrine taught by us many years ago. For nearly thirty years we have taught that sectarianism was anti-Christian, and that all Christians should be united in one body of Christ— the same they teach. We then and ever since, have taught that authoritative creeds and confessions were the strong props of sectarianism, and should be given to the moles and bats—they teach the same. We have from that time preached the gospel to every creature to whom we have access, and urged them to believe and obey it—that its own evidence was sufficient to produce faith in all that heard it, that the unrenewed sinner must, and could, believe it unto justification and salvation—and that through faith the Holy Spirit of promise, and every other promise of the New Covenant, were given. They proclaim the same doctrine. Many years ago, some of us preached baptism as a means, in connexion with faith and repentance, for the remission of sins, and the gift of the Holy Spirit—they preach the same, and extend it farther than we have done. We rejected all names but Christians—they acknowledge it most proper, but seem to prefer another." (Charles Crossfield Ware, Life of Stone, pp. 226- 227. Quotation from Stone's paper, "Christian Messenger.")

"The practice of immersion soon prevailed very generally among the churches, and even its design appeared to have been at one time dimly recognized by Mr. Stone." (J.H. Milburn, Origin of Campbellism, p. 69.)

1801 "... At a great meeting at Concord . « . ,the words of Peter at Pentecost,' says he (Stone) 'rolled through my mind'; 'Repent and be baptized for the remission of sins, and ye shall receive the gift of the Holy Spirit.' I thought were Peter here he would thus address these mourners. I quickly arose and addressed them in the same language, and urged them to comply." (Richardson, Memoirs of Campbell, II, 197.)

"They (Stone et al) apply the appelation 'Christians' to their churches and call themselves 'Christians' exclusively and claim to have no creed but the Bible; thus they did years before Campbellism started and this they do yet." (J.T. Milburn, Origin of Campbellism, p. 80.)

STONE SAID "... My mind has been long in the belief that weekly communion was according to truth." (A.W. Fortune, The Disciples in Kentucky, p. 61.)

"They decided henceforth to be known as Christians only. In this action they were influenced by Rev. Rice Haggard, a colaborer of Rev. James O'Kelley,... Haggard had recently come to Kentucky, was present at the meeting of the Presbytery of Springfield in 1804, and suggested the name Christian as having been 'given to the disciples by divine appointment, first at Antioch'." (Frank G. Beardsley, Christianity in America, p. 104.)

"Further augmented by secession from the Baptists in New England by Dr. Abner Jones, who, rejecting all party names and desiring to be known only as a Christian. ... In Kentucky the followers of Stone were denominated the 'Newlights,' a name which they always disclaimed, preferring to be known only as Christians." (Frank G. Beardsley, ibid., pp. 104-105.)

"Coming in contact with Barton W. Stone and the 'Newlight' Christians of Kentucky, Alexander Campbell found that they had many things in common and a partial union was effected at Lexington, Ky., in 1832." (Ibid., p. 146.)

'When the doctrinal views of Barton W. Stone and those of Alexander Campbell were brought to a comparison... there were so many points of agreement that a union between the two sects was soon proposed. To carry the proposal into effect, a great mass-meeting, composed of members of both sects, was held in Lexington, January 1, 1832." (J.H. Spencer, A History of the Kentucky Baptists, p. 526, 527.)

"Other religious movements, too, had been for some time operating to weaken the power of sectarianism and to restore the Bible to its proper position... The religious body to which they (Stone et al) belonged, bad an earlier origin than that which sprung from Mr. Campbell's labors." (Richardson. Memoirs of Campbell, II, 182-183.)

"They (Campbell et al) were fully assured of the righteousness of their cause, and as confident of the near approach of the Millennium, as McNemar, Dunlavy, Stone and their coadjutors had been twenty-seven years before." (J.H. Spencer, A History of the Kentucky Baptists, p. 617.)

"The marble shaft which marks his burial place bears the following inscription: The Church of Christ at Cane Ridge, and other generous friends in Kentucky have caused this monument to be erected as a tribute of affection and gratitude to Barton W. Stone." (A.W. Fortune, The Disciple in Kentucky, p. 32.)

SOME OLD LETTERS

"Mt. Vernon (Ilk), January 15, 1823.

"I, James Smith, one of the elders of the Christian church, do hereby certify that our beloved brother, John

Whitmire, and sister Elizabeth Whitmire, his wife, were members of the aforesaid church in good standing, and reputed as acceptable brethren among (us) in the bonds of Christian union, until their removal from this county about two years ago, (1821). As such we hope the brethren will receive and consider them—James Smith, Elder and Secretary of the church at Licking." (From an original letter owned by his son-in-law, Alatt Hale, Grandview, Texas.)

"This certifies that again after a careful search of all records and by careful inquiry among the oldest members, one who has belonged to the church for seventy years;... that the church here is at least 120 years of age. In the oldest record opposite two names, one has this entry: Baptized 1811; at another place, died Oct. 5th, 1818. The date 1819 appears in two separate places. The first house of worship was built about 1820. In the year 1827 we find that the church here had five elders. Speaking of this congregation, in an issue of the Gospel Advocate in June, 1902. David Lipscomb said: 'This is the oldest congregation now in existence and was planted by Barton W. Stone and his associates in the early part of the last century, who planted many churches along the mountain bench of Kentucky, Tennessee and Alabama.' ... It has always been a rule here to teach the Bible and the Bible only. We still teach and practice here at the church of Christ at Rocky Springs, what our forebears did over 100 years ago. ...

A COPY OF A LETTER RECEIVED BY THIS CHURCH

'State of Tennessee, Warren County,
'Oct. 22, 1818
"The church of Christ at Philadelphia commends to the fellowship of the faithful in Christ Jesus our beloved sister Elizabeth Brown, as a faithful member in the Kingdom of Christ Jesus. George Stroud, David Ramsay, Bishops."
'Yours in Christ, A.B. Adams, J.C. Adams, A.J. Aren-

dale, ELDERS.

'W.E. Arendale, DEACON.

'L. EL Hughes, MEMBER HOUSE OE REPRESENTATIVES.J. R. Loyd, Bridgeport, Alabama. Sworn to and subscribed before me this Nov. 7, 1927. W.R. Bogart, JUDGE PROBATE."

In the Firm Foundation, Austin, Texas, May 16, 1939, Guy N. Woods, a reliable and recognized preacher of the church of Christ gave an article, quoting at length from "Primitive Christian and Investigator," a paper published at Auburn, N.Y., from 1835 to 1839 by Silas E. Shepherd who wrote under the sub-title "Extract from a Serious Reply to the Rev. John Wesley, by Gilbert Boyce, a Baptist"—titled, "Campbellism About a Century Ago," Vol. 1836. According to Mr. Shepherd, this Mr. Boyce, a Baptist, over two hundred years ago, said: "Baptism is necessary to penitent believers to entitle them to the promise of forgiveness of sins, which is freely given to all such through the redemption which they have in Christ (Eph. 1:7). Accordingly, Saint Peter says to his new-made converts at Jerusalem, 'Repent and be baptized every one of you in the name of Jesus Christ, for the remission of sins' (Acts 2:38). It ought to be observed that the remission of sins is not promised to repentance only, but to repentance and baptism. The apostle seems to make baptism as necessary as repentance, to entitle them to the promise; not to either of them singly and separately from one another, but to both conjointly. Therefore, it appears plain that baptism is to be an inseparable companion with repentance, as faith is to be with them both, in order to receive the promise." That shows that many did not know any better than to accept the plain teachings of the Scriptures on any and all subjects until they were taught against the plain truths. That also shows that all who taught immersion in water was Scriptural baptism were called baptists in history. But I want to give one more to confirm the above statement.

A Handbook of Historical Briefs

"An incident occurred in the Pilot Point (Texas) (Baptist) church during Rev. J.B. Cole's pastorate, which involved a point of doctrine that subjected Pastor Cole to criticism, and gave the incident much publicity and notoriety. Pastor Cole went fishing one day with a business man who was not a Christian, and he availed himself of the opportunity to talk to the lost man about his unsaved condition, and led him to an acceptance of Christ. Jo Ives, the man converted, said to Pastor Cole,

'Here is water, what doth hinder me from being baptized?' Obviously, Brother Cole thought of the story of Philip and the eunuch, and, taking that incident as an example, he led Mr. Ives out into the water and baptized him. Rev. Cole had been a Baptist but a short time and was not up on their conception of baptism, and how and when it should be administered. The news of the incident soon spread among the members, and then the show began. The following Sunday Mr. Ives presented himself to the church, asking membership, and his application was rejected and he was hurt at the action of the church and turned to another church, which readily accepted his baptism. The criticism of the pastor caused him to ask a committee of eminent brethren to sit in judgment upon his conduct—Drs. A.J. Holt, J.B. Link and R.C. Buckner. After receiving the details of the incident, they wrote the church advising it to drop the matter, and Pastor Cole to go his way, but not to repeat the act." (James Newton Rayzor, History of Denton County Texas Baptist Associations, pp. 82-83.) In this connection read Acts 8:36-39.

CHAPTER 7
BAPTISTS IN AMERICA

When, where and how the church of Christ was connected with this history.

THOMAS CAMPBELL

"While yet in Scotland, the Campbell's, and especially Thomas (For Alexander was not yet out of his teens), were impressed with the necessity and desirability of discussing Christian union by an appeal to the word of God, and this necessity and desirability was impressed upon his mind by the 'Haldaneon Reformation." (Jno. R. Rowe, Reformatory Movement, p. 128.)

"It will be seen, further, that the positions taken by the Christian Association at this period were almost identical with those held by the churches established by the Haldanes." (Richardson, Memoirs of Campbell, I, 349.)

"The antecendants of Thomas and Alexander Campbell, including their connection with Scottish sects, and the manifest influence of Sandmanianism on their modes of religious thoughts...." (A. H. Newman, History of the Baptist Churches in the United States, p. 488.)

"In August, 1809, he (Thomas) organized his followers into the 'Christian Association' of Washington (County), Pennsylvania;... deploring human creeds and systems ... holding that they should follow the example of the New Testament church." (Frank G. Beardsley, Christianity in America, p. 145.)

"The allusion to Elder Thomas Campbell is particularly fine, and not more elegant and felicitous than true. For he, beyond all question, first settled upon the great principle—the seed—truth from all that is valuable in the Reformation sprung —'That we must speak where the Scriptures speak, and be silent where they are silent'; or, in other , words, make the Word of God the only rule of faith and practice." (William Baxter, Life of Walter Scott, p. 116.)

"Thomas Campbell having moved to Pittsburg, Pa., and from thence to Kentucky, and from thence back to Western Pennsylvania; again resumed the pastoral care of the Brush Run church. The biographer says: 'He, himself, spent the most of his time at his son, Alexander's; about seven miles distant, in assisting to conduct school; and he resumed the pastoral care of the Brush Run church, which he had planted some ten years before." (J.H. Milburn, Origin of Campbellism, p. 38.)

"Thomas Campbell sowed the germ thought of the Current Reformation in the terse saying: (1809. J.P.W.) 'Where the Scriptures speak, we speak; and where the Scriptures are silent we are silent' Memoirs of Campbell, Vol I, p. 236. The Reformation movement is dated from the time the above words were spoken." (D.N. Jackson, "Origin of the Campbellite Church," The American Baptist, September 26, 1942, ed. D.N. Jackson.)

"The writing with which he (Thomas Campbell) was at this time engaged was a "Declaration and Address," .... When this was finished, he called a special meeting of the chief members and read it to them for their approval and adoption. Having been unanimously agreed to, it was at once ordered to be printed, September 7, 1809." (Richardson, Memoirs of Campbell, I, pp. 241, 242.)

"As late as 1831 Thomas Campbell was received into many Baptist pulpits and heard by Semple and Broadus during a trip to Virginia." (Gates and Hulbert, The Early Relations and Separation of Baptists and Disciples, p. 102.)

ALEXANDER CAMPBELL

"Thomas and Alexander, his son, with five others of the family rejected infant baptism, and on June 12, 1812, were immersed on profession of their faith in Christ, in Buffalo Creek, by Elder Luce, and were received into the fellowship of the Brush Run Baptist church." (Thomas Armitage, History of the Baptists, p. 735.)

"He used these memorable words to Loos, the Baptist minister, who baptized him: 'I have set out to follow the apostles of Christ, and their Master, and I will be baptized only in the primitive Christian faith." (Hurst, Short History of the Christian Church, p. 558.)

"In 1812, he was immersed by Elder Luce, a Baptist minister, without the action or authority of any Baptist church, and contrary to invariable and recognized law and usage of Baptist churches." (J.R. Graves, Trilemma, p. 191.)

"Alexander had stipulated with Elder Luce that the ceremony should be performed precisely according to the pattern given in the New Testament, and that there was no account of any of the first converts being called to give what is called a 'religious experience.' This modern custom should be omitted, and that the candidates should be admitted on the simple confession that 'Jesus is the Son of God.' Elder Luce had, indeed, at first objected to these changes, as being contrary to Baptist usages, but finally consented, remarking that he believed they were right, and he would run the risk of censure." (Ibid., p. 192.)

GARBLED EXTRACTS

"Mr. Luce had no authority to baptize Mr. Campbell, and therefore the immersion he performed in Buffalo Creek was not Christian baptism ... MR. CAMPBELL NEVER WAS BAPTIZED. He says: 'Remission of sins can not be enjoyed by any person before immersion. Belief of this testimony is what impelled us into the water, knowing that the efficacy of his blood is to be communicated to our consciences in the way which God has pleased to appoint. We stagger not at the promise, but flee to the sacred ordinance (water of baptism) which brought the blood of Jesus in contact with our consciences. WITHOUT KNOWING AND

BELIEVING THIS, IMMERSION IS A BLASTED NUT-THE SHELL IS THERE, BUT THE KERNEL IS WANTING.' Christian Baptism, p. 521." (J.R. Graves, Trilemma, pp. 194-195.) (His emphasis, J.P. W.)

NOTE! Having seen so many garbled extracts of this statement from brother Campbell, from the small fry among Baptist et al writers and debaters, I decided, since they hardly ever read any thing but that which is put out by their own sect, that I would at least give them a chance to act fair and quote Campbell correct one time. I am inserting exactly what he did say in answer to a question, and which Graves here only attempts to quote, and most of them get theirs from Graves, I am sure. THIS IS WHAT AN HONEST READER WILL SEE IN CAMPBELL'S WORK CALLED THE CHRISTIAN BAPTIST, p. 521:

"QUERY VII. Is it, or is it not, through faith in the blood of Jesus Christ, that we receive the remission of our sins in the act of immersion? ANSWER. I had thought that in my Essays on Immersion this point was fully settled. Every single blessing, and all blessings collectively, appertaining to salvation, flow to us from the sacrifice of Jesus the Son of God. (Garblers always leave the above out, J.P. W.) The value and efficacy of his sacrifice is the very document itself which constitutes the burthen of the testimony. Belief of this testimony is what impells us into the water. Knowing that the efficacy of this blood is to be communicated to our consciences in the way which God has pleased to appoint, we 'stagger not at the promise of God,' but flee to the sacred ordinance which brings the blood of Jesus in contact with our consciences. Without knowing and believing this, immersion is as empty as a blasted nut. The shell is there, but the kernel is wanting... But this always connected with faith in the blood of Jesus Christ, which blood is the only consideration in the universe worthy of the bestowment of such blessings upon the children of men." (Alexander Campbell, Christian Baptist, p. 521.)

I HERE GIVE OTHER GARBLED EXTRACTS OF THE ABOVE STATEMENT BY BROTHER CAMPBELL. "Remission of sins cannot be enjoyed by any person before immersion... Without knowing and believing this, immersion is a blasted nut—the shell is there, but the kernel is wanting. (Christian Baptism, p. 531.)" (D.N. Jackson, "Origin of the Campbellite Church," American Baptist, December 24, 1942, ed. D.N. Jackson.) He also quotes this in the Smith Debate, p. 85.)

"Christian Baptism, page 531 he says: 'Remission of sins cannot be enjoyed by any person before immersion... Without knowing and believing this, immersion is a blasted nut—the shell is there but the kernel is wanting.'" (Dr. J.E. Cobb, Baptist, in the "American Baptist," a paper printed in 1942. His 8th affirmative, in the "Cobb-Wilhite Debate.")

Again, "Remission of sins cannot be enjoyed by any person before immersion.... Without knowing and believing this, immersion is a blasted nut—the shell is there, but the kernel is wanting... (Christian Baptist, p. 53.)" (He says "page 53" instead on page 531, J.P. W.) (J.W. Kesner, Sr., Campbellism Exposed, Article by Vernon Barr, p. 84.)

Once more, "Remission of sins cannot be enjoyed by any person before immersion. Belief of this testimony is what impelled us into the water, knowing that the efficacy of his blood is to be communicated to our consciences in the way God has pleased to appoint: we stagger not at the promise but flee to the sacred ordinance which brought the blood of Jesus in contact with our consciences. Without knowing and believing this, immersion is a blasted nut, the shell is there, but the kernel is wanting." (William Nevins, Alien Baptism and the Baptists, p. 24.)

"He should not slander any man especially the dead." (Dr. D.N. Jackson Debate with Roy Cogdill, Am. Bap., 12/15/48.)

My honest opinion concerning these garbled extracts, and maybe many others, is that their APOSTLE Graves, set the example and others copied from him, without reading the original from the pen of the author. The reader will notice that each of these Baptist men quote from Campbell, the first phrase, "Remission of sins cannot be enjoyed by any person before immersion," which is NOT TO BE FOUND IN CAMPBELL'S words where they pretend to quote. THAT PART IS NOT THERE. Since they all use it alike, they are bound to be copying from each other. Jackson used it on at least two different occasions, as cited above. Each quotation I have cited is exact, even in punctuations. Graves and Nevins do not even give signs that there is a skip in his words. Kesner, Jackson and Barr do. Graves and Jackson say it is found in "Christian Baptism," Jackson in both his history and the Smith debate, as does Cobb also. Gentlemen, it is found in "Christian Baptist," as Barr and Kesner says. Nevins doesn't even cite the book. Jackson says he is quoting from page 531 in both places he is quoted, so does Cobb. Kesner and Barr say it is on page 53, while Graves gives the correct page number, but each of them have garbled and misrepresented the dead—simply take advantage of a dead man. If they will misrepresent in one place, they will in any case they consider to their sectarian advantage. If not, why not?

Furthermore, I want to call your attention to the fact that these men, although supposed to be men of fame among modern Baptists, and defenders of their faith, have left the wrong impressions on their readers in each case. They tell us that Campbell said, "Remission of sins cannot be enjoyed by any person before immersion. Belief of this testimony is what impelled us into the water" etc. Campbell did not say that. These statements are not connected by Campbell in this quotation at all. Campbell said, "Every single blessing, and all blessings collectively, appertaining to salvation, FLOW TO US FROM THE SACRIFICE OF JESUS THE SON OF GOD. THE VALUE AND EFFICACY OF HIS SACRIFICE IS THE VERY DOCUMENT

ITSELF WHICH CONSTITUTES THE BURTHEN OF THE TESTIMONY. BELIEF OF THIS TESTIMONY IS WHAT IMPELLS US INTO THE WATER." (My caps, J.P. W.) Any one can see the difference. Garblers make it ALL depend on WATER, while brother Campbell made it ALL depend upon Christ, and His sacrifice, to the ones who will do what he says regardless of what that is. This exposure seemed necessary, since they do this all the time and every where they attempt to answer us.

"In 1812 he accepted baptism by immersion at the hands of the Baptist Elder Luce... They were Baptists now, not 'Campbellites' as the frontiers had called them." (Frank S. Mead, See These Banners Go, p. 260.)

"If Mr. McCalla would enter into the discussion, I would engage to show that baptism, as viewed and practiced by the Baptists, had its advocates in every century up to the Christian era... That all the writers of the first and second centuries, inspired and uninspired, speak of a believer as the only subject, and of immersion as the only baptism. In the third century infant baptism was introduced, but only in certain cases... hosts in the sixteenth century have advocated the Baptists sentiments and practice... clouds of witnesses attest the fact, that before the Reformation from Popery, and from the apostolic age to the present time, the sentiment of Baptists, and the practice of baptism, have had a continued chain of advocates, and public monuments of their existence in every century can be produced." (Campbell-McCalla Debate, new ed. pp. 338-339, old ed. p. 378.)

I shall show you some GARBLERS QUOTES TO MISLEAD ON THE ABOVE STATEMENTS. "From the apostolic age to the present time, the sentiments of Baptists have had a continued chain of advocates, and public monuments of their existence in every century can be produced." (J.W. Kesner, Sr., Campbellism Exposed, Art. by Vernon Barr, p. 46.) Here Barr and Kesner mislead so that the reader cannot tell that he is actually speaking of what is sometimes called the MODE of baptism, and nor of the Baptists as a denomination. I agree that some have advocated immersion of believers. But Barr and Kesner left out five words near the middle of the quotation, hence garbled.

Again, "From the apostolic age to the present time the sentiments of Baptists and their practice of baptism have had a continued chain of advocates, and public monuments of their existence in every century can be produced." (J.E. Cobb, Wilhite- Cobb Debate, II, 5.) (Immersionists all the way.)

Again, Dr. D.N. Jackson adds a few words to the above quotation as follows: "Clouds of witnesses attest the fact, that before the Reformation from Popery, and from the apostolic age. . . etc., which is also misleading. (D.N. Jackson, Reasons for Being a Baptist, p. 13.)

Once more, here is what Ben Bogard says of Campbell's work on Baptism, p. 409. He said, "From the apostolic age to the present time the sentiments of Baptists and their practice of baptism has had a continued chain of advocates, and public monuments of their existence in every century can be produced." (Porter-Bogard Debate, p. 154.) So you see Bogard not only misapplies the statement, but cites as reference an entirely different book. I am showing you how we are misrepresented by these little fellows.

How do I know what Campbell meant? Well, he said: "The Baptists, as now distinguished from other Protestant parties, began since the Protestant Reformation;... About the middle of the seventeenth century (1643) seven churches in London, and afterwards (July 7, 1689) about one hundred churches in England and Wales, met in London and fully set forth their faith and opinions in the form of a 'Confession,' of which I have the ninth American edition— Philadelphia, 1798—adopted by the Baptist Association met in Philadelphia, September 25, 1742. From this document and its history, we can give to the Baptist denomination a habitation and a name two hundred years old." (Millennial Harbinger, ed. Campbell, a religious journal, Vol. 5, 1841.) That would make him say they started about 1641.

WHAT IS A BAPTIST ANYWAY? "Faith publicly expressed, by a voluntary submission to his authority and doctrine in baptism. Wherever this conduct is evident, we claim the disciple as belonging to our communion and of primitive character." (Orchard, A Concise History of the Foreign Baptists, by J.R. Graves, Introduction, p. 14.)

CHAPTER 8
BAPTISTS CLAIMED CAMPBELL

"By his fearless and forceable defense of the distinctive sentiments of the Baptists, in his debate with Messrs. Walker and McCalla, he secured extensively the confidence and esteem of the (Baptist) denomination. They were proud to acknowledge him as the bold and puisant champion of their cause." (J.B. Jeter, Campbellism Examined, p. 76.)

"It had happened, during the fall of 1819, that a Mr. John Birch, a Baptist preacher at Flat Rock, near Mt. Pleasant, Ohio, had baptized an unusual number of converts... (The Presbyterians challenged him for a debate because of that, and he secured Alexander Campbell to represent the side on immersion, Campbell was reluctant, so Birch wrote him the second time stating): I can truly say it is the unanimous wish of all the church to which I belong that you should be the disputant". So it was arranged and held, beginning June 19, 1820. (Richardson, Memoirs of Campbell, II, 14-16.)

So, at that time the Baptists claimed Mr. Campbell as a Baptist. What did he teach in his debate in 1820? Here it is:

"'Baptism,' said he, 'is connected with the promise of the remission of sins and the gift of the Holy Spirit.' This utterance is worthy of notice as his first definite and public recognition of the peculiar office of baptism." (Ibid., II, 20.)

"The Ohio river, in the beginning of October, 1823, being too low for steamboat navigation, Mr. Campbell was compelled to set out on horseback in order to meet his appointment with Mr. McCalla in Kentucky." (Ibid., II, 71.) In this debate, as he again met the Presbyterians, he used Mark 16:16; John 3:5; Acts 2:38; 1 Cor. 6:11; Acts 22:16; Tit. 3:5 and 1 Pet. 3:21 in defence of baptism, but some of these modern Baptists say they do not refer to baptism, and at least some say some of them are not inspired. After telling them neither Baptists nor Pedabaptists sufficiently appreciate it, saying, "Never was there an ordinance of so great import or design," and arguing the Bible design so strongly, he said, "I know it will be said that I have affirmed that baptism SAVES us. Well, Peter and Paul have said so before me. If it was not criminal in them to say so, it cannot be criminal in me." (Ibid., II, 81.)

"Sidney Rigdon and Walter Scott both attended the discussion between Mr. Campbell and Mr. McCalla, and heard proclaimed publicly for the first time the doctrine of baptism in order to the remission of past sins." (J. H. Milburn, Origin of Campbellism, p. 47.)

Remember the Baptists claimed him as a Baptist at that time.

"It is a redeeming quality in Campbellism that it uniformly professes a profound respect for the teaching of the Bible. Air. Campbell holds many, and most important principles, in common with all Christians. Nobly did he vindicate the authenticity and inspiration of the Scriptures, and the vital principles of Christianity, in his debate with Robert Owen, of Scotland, the champion of infidelity; and by that service entitled himself to the gratitude and commendation of the friends of morality and social order. Mr. Campbell holds many truths in common with all Protestants; and in his discussion with Bishop Purcell, of the Romish communion, maintained them with signal ability, and fully justified his claim to be classed among the able defenders of Protestantism... Mr. Campbell embraces some views in common with Baptists. Whatever evil he may have done them, directly and indirectly—and they have been neither few nor small—he should have due praise for his indefatigable efforts to restore the apostolic baptism, or the immersion of believers, to expose the traditionary origin of infant baptism, and to show that the primitive churches were composed exclusively of baptized believers." (J.B. Jeter, Campbellism Examined, pp. 114-115.)

The debate with Owens took place in the year 1829, and the Baptists still claimed him, as you can see; but that isn't all.

"The Western states, within a few years past, have been the most distinguished for baptismal controversies, and Campbell and Waller on the side of the Baptists, and Rice and—for the pedobaptists." (David Benedict, History of the Baptists, p. 280.) That debate was held in 1843. When they thought that he did good, the Baptists still claimed him.

He said "I had no idea of uniting with the Baptists, more than with the Moravians or the mere Independents." (Richardson, Memoirs of Campbell, f, 438.)

"The Reformers belong to the Baptist family." (J.B. Jeter, Campbellism Examined, p. 359.)

"They do, it is true, insist that their members shall speak of Bible things in Bible terms. To restore a pure, or Scriptural speech, is one of the main objects of the Reformation for which Mr. Campbell pleads." (Ibid., p. 35.)

"His personality was the most vigorous type, and for over a generation his name was a tower of strength over the whole United States...." (Hurst, Short History of the Christian Church, p. 557.)

"'The Holy Spirit,' he affirms, 'is not promised to any person outside of Christ.' This position I do not controvert." (Jeter, op. cit., p. 168.)

"Mr. Campbell has been frequently, but, I think, unfairly charged with teaching baptismal regeneration." (Ibid., p. 197.)

"The Baptist society invited Mr. Campbell to make a translation of the book of Acts for their version (American Bible Union Version, J.P. W.) which he did." (A.T. DeGroot, Three Fourths of a Loaf, a tract reprinted in "The Chronicle," Baptist Historical Quarterly, April 1948, p. 3)

"The Baptists, too, it must be admitted, are not precisely what they would have been, had there been no Reformation." (J.B. Jeter, Campbellism Examined, p. 368.)

They were "devastating the (Baptist, J.P. W.) churches in this region of the state as a tornado sweeps away the forest in its track." (J.H. Spencer, History of the Baptists in Kentucky, p. 37.)

"OTHER BAPTISTS. ... The Disciples of Christ, sometimes called Campbellites, or Christians, number about 1,200,000." (Hiscox, Standard Baptist Church Manual, p. 174.)

"I have found objections on both sides against placing this society among the branches of the great Baptist family; but as they hold to two great primordial principles of all Baptists, viz., IMMERSION on a PROFESSION OF FAITH, and are thorough going anti-pedobaptists, without any formal permission from either my own people, or my QUONDAM or QUASI brethren, on my own responsibility, as they are BAPTISTS DE FACTO, 1 shall regard them as such in my statistical accounts." (David Benedict, History of the Baptists, p. 916.)

"He (Mr. Campbell, J.P. W.) sought membership of his church in the Red Stone Baptist Association." (Dr. D.N. Jackson, Origin of Campbellite Church, The American Baptist, ed. by D.N. Jack- son, November 23, 1942.)

"In addition to his acquaintance with Messrs. Luce and Speers, Mr. Campbell had, from time to time, formed that of other members belonging to the (Redstone) Association, who often urged that the Brush Run church should connect itself with this religious body... although the Brush Run members had adopted immersion, and were hence reputed to be Baptists, they felt that there was a wide difference between them and the Baptist communities in regards to the great principles of religious liberty and progress, as well as the necessity of returning to the faith and practice of the primitive churches... They often sent for us and pressed us to preach for them." (Richardson, Memoirs of Campbell, I, 436-440.)

A Handbook of Historical Briefs

"Alexander Campbell was a man of fair education and of unbounded confidence in his resources and his tenets. He was possessed of a powerful personality and was one of the ablest debaters of his age." (A.I. Newman, History of the Baptist Churches in the United States, p. 489.)

"It has already been stated that it was not Mr. Campbell's purpose—certainly not his avowed purpose—to form a new sect, but to abolish all sects." (J.B. Jeter, Campbellism Examined, p. 83.)

"I have no idea of adding to the catalog of new sects. ... I labor to see sectarianism abolished and all Christians of every name united upon the one foundation upon which the apostolic church was founded. To bring Baptists and Pedobaptists to ibis is my supreme end." (Richardson, Memoirs of Campbell, II, 135.)

"'I would not, sir, value at the price of a single mill, the religion of any man, as respects the grand affair of eternal life, whose religion is not begun, carried on, and completed by the personal agency of the Holy Spirit.'" (J.B. Jeter, Campbellism Examined, p. 180, quoted from Campbell-Rice Debate, p. 614.)

"1 believe the Spirit accompanies the word, is always present with the word, and ACTUALLY AND PERSONALLY works through it upon the moral nature of man, but not without it.'" (Ibid., quoted from Campbell-Rice Debate, p. 745.)

"No man believes more cordially, or teaches more fully, the necessity of a spiritual change of our affections—a change of heart—than I do. I have said a thousand times, that if a person were to be immersed twice seven times in the Jordan for the remission of his sins, or for the reception of the Holy Spirit, it would avail nothing more than wetting the face of a babe, unless his heart is changed by the word and Spirit of God.'" (Ibid., p. 192, quoted from "Campbell-Rice Debate," p. 544.)

"Infants, idiots, deaf and dumb persons, innocent Pagans where ever they be found, with all the pious pedo-Baptists, we commend to the mercy of God." (J.H. Milburn, Origin of Campbellism, p. 93, quoted from the "Christian System.")

"The bride of Christ will not be made up of all the saved... but she will be made up of all those who are saved and have identified themselves in a real sense of the term with the Lord's true church." (p. 30.) (That means only Baptists will thus be honored and that because they have been BAPTIZED by a Baptist preacher, J.P. W.) "All the saved who are not part of the bride will be there as guests." (D.N. Jackson, Ten Reasons Why I Am A Baptist, p. 32.) In other words, you can't get all the enjoyment of heaven, even if you do creep in, unless you have been baptized—and that by a Baptist preacher. This theory is not even hinted at in the Bible—that some get hell in heaven, because they were not baptized by a Baptist preacher.

"No intelligent Christian can object to the end which Mr. C. proposed to accomplish." (J.B. Jeter, Campbellism Examined, p. 22.)

"I had no idea of uniting with the Baptists," said A. Campbell. (Mem. of Camp. Vol. I, p. 438.)

"Mr. Campbell's influence was so great, both in the church of which he was a member, and the small association to which he belonged, that, notwithstanding his known and publicly avowed heterodoxy, neither had he been disciplined by his church for heresy, nor his church by its association for retaining him as a member. The Baptist denomination was, therefore, held responsible for his teaching.... In August, 1829, Beaver Association, a small Baptist fraternity in Pennsylvania, met at Providence meetinghouse, near Pittsburg... resolved to withdraw fellowship from Mahoning Association, on account of its maintaining, or countenancing, the following sentiments, or creed: 1. They maintained that there is no promise of salvation without baptism. ... 3. That there is no direct operation of the

Holy Spirit, on the mind, prior to baptism. ... 5. That the Scriptures are the only evidence of interest in Christ. 6. That obedience places it in God's power to elect to salvation. 7. That no creed is necessary for the church but the Scriptures as they stand... This is believed to have been the first official declaration of non-fellowship for Mr. Campbell and his followers." (J.H. Spencer, A History of the Kentucky Baptists, pp. 609 and 610.)

So far as we know, Campbell was never in the above Association, much less ever being a member of it, but you can see how they once loved this man, and how later, because he stood for truth, and "Scriptures as they stand" they unlawfully, according to their own views, pretended to turn him out. This was the only way to deal with him.

"Mr. (J.R.) Graves, in the standing column of the Baptists, says: 'that a body of immersed believers is the highest ecclesiastical authority in the world, and the only tribunal for the trial of cases of discipline; that the acts of a church are of superior binding force over those of an Association... and no Association or Convention can impose a moral obligation upon the constituent parts composing them." (D.B. Ray, Baptist Church Succession, p. 224.) The withdrawal was all humbugery, and no living man can find where any church ever turned Alexander Campbell out for heresy or for any other reason. (J.P. W.)

As early as 1826, "Some religious editors in Kentucky call those who are desirous of seeing the ancient order of things restored, 'The Restorationers', 'The Campbellites.'" (Mr. Campbell protested against the designation of Campbellites.) (The Christian Baptist, ed. by Campbell, p. 288.)

"About the first of March 1826, Spencer Clack and George Waller commenced the publication, at Bloomfield, Kentucky, of a periodical, under the style of 'Baptist Register,' the name of which was soon afterwards exchanged for that of the 'Baptist Recorder.' The object of the publication seems to have been to expose the errors advocated by Alexander Campbell... that system of doctrine which had already been designated by the title of 'Campbellism.'" (J.H. Spencer, History of the Kentucky Baptists, p. 597.)

CHAPTER 9
HUMAN CREEDS

Human creeds, which resulted in man organized Associations and the effect upon the religious conditions.

"Primitive Christianity drew up no Confessions of Faith... The earliest is the so-called Apostles' Creed... Traces of this creed can be found as early as A.D.200 (W.J. McGlothlin, Baptist Confessions of Faith, intro, p. 9.)

"Creed-making now ceased for nearly a thousand years, (Dark Age Period, J.P. W.) till the beginning of the theological controversies aroused by the Reformation. Beginning with the Augsburg Confession in 1530." (W.J. McGlothlin, Ibid., intro, p. 10.)

FIRST BAPTIST CREED IN ENGLISH, AS PRINTED IN THAT DAY: "upon everie first day off the weeke, being the LORD'S day, to assemble together to pray Prophecie, praise GOD, and break Bread." (Ibid, p. 90.)

"Roger Williams,... First Church of Providence, the earliest Baptist church in America. At that date there was no Calvinistic Baptist Confession in existence. The church drew up none, and has continued to this day without any statement of doctrine." (W.J. McGlothlin, Baptist Confessions of Faith, p. 293.)

"There were other Baptist churches that rejected all human creeds. This was true of the Separate churches especially. Such churches were, of course, very cordial toward the teaching of Campbell." (Gates and Hulbert, The Early Relations and Separation of Baptists and Disciples, p. 82.)

"September 25th, 1742,... the first of this (Philadelphia Baptist Confession) or any other Baptist Confession to be printed in America...." (W.J. McGlothlin, Baptist Confessions of Faith, p. 295.)

"The New Lights (Some times called Separatists, J.P. W.) published an apology... they maintained that all creeds and confessions ought to be rejected, and that the Bible alone, without note or comment, should be the bond of Christian fellowship." (J.H. Spencer, A History of the Kentucky Baptists, p. 524.)

"It was the infusion of the Separates among the Baptist churches of Kentucky, Virginia, and Tennessee that furthered the propagation of the principles of the Reformers among them in those states." (Gates and Hulbert, The Early Relations and Separation of Baptists and Disciples, p. 79.)

STONE AND OTHER "seceding ministers in their opposition to creeds and authoritative ecclesiastical systems... They stated their objections to the Confessions of Faith, and their abandonment of every thing but the Bible as the rule of faith and practice." (J.H. Milburn, Origin of Campbellism, p. 68.)

"The so-called New Hampshire Confession of Faith. ... It is perhaps the most widely used and influential statement of doctrine among American Baptists at the present time...." (W.J. McGlothlin, Baptist Confessions of Faith, p. 299.)

"In 1867, Rev. J.M. Pendleton, who was then pastor of Upland, Pa., incorporated this Confession in his Church Manual." (W.J. McGlothlin, Baptist Confessions of Faith, p. 301.)

"In 1890, Rev. E.T. Hiscox, in his 'Standard Manual,' divided the article on 'Baptism and the Lord's Supper' into two, making nineteen articles in all." (Ibid., p. 301.)

AMERICAN BAPTIST TRAINING COURSE: "AMERICAN B.T. C. IS FORMED" (Dr. D.N. Jackson, American Baptist, 9/13/41.1

"I started the B.T. C. work among our people and in December 1918 I wrote the first B.T. C. Quarterly ever published among us. Was that a failure?" (Ibid., March 12, 1947.)

ASSOCIATIONS

"WHAT IS AN ASSOCIATION?... THERE IS NO TRIBUNAL HIGHER THAN A CHURCH." (His Caps, J.P. W.) (Dr. D.N. Jackson, ed. American Baptist October 1, 1946.)

"Churches in good order may be received into the membership, (of an Association, J.P. W.) upon application by letter and messengers, presenting such Articles of Faith, (CREED, J.P. W.) adopted by them, as shall be acceptable to this body." (J.N. Rayzor, History of the Denton Co. Texas Baptist Association, p. 120.)

"It is in accordance with Baptist principles for such a body to make its own terms of membership." (W.P. Throgmorton, Missionary Baptist, Throgmorton-Potter Debate, in 1887 on "Who Are the Primitive Baptists?" publishing committee, J.N. Hall and J.H. Milburn, Missionary Baptists and Dr. H.C. Roberts and Dr. S.F. Cayce, Primitive Baptists, p. 15.)

"We pretend no divine authority or positive precept for associations, but consider them as resulting from general principles of expediency...." (Theology and History, quoted from "Minutes of Central Union Association, of Penn, Baptist Publication, p. 6.)

"Where have you any authority for Associations? There is no authority in the Bible for any of these things; and if you practice them, you practice something that is not laid down in the law." This was spoken by Mr. Wallace, the Missionary Baptist, in a debate with what is sometimes called Hardshell, or Primitive, to which Mr. Hardy the Primitive Baptist asked: "Well, don't you do it, too?" The Missionary Baptist said, "Yes, but I am talking to you now. You claim that you do nothing but what is in the Bible. There is the difference between us. We do not pretend to look to the Bible for authority for everything we do." (Hardy-Wallace Debate, pp. 252-253, 1880.)

"There are some things which both Hardshells and Missionaries hold and practice for which there is no direct New Testament precept or example... holding of annual associations... Moderator and clerk, the motion and second..." (Throgmorton-Potter Debate, 1887, p. 5.) (Spoken by Throgmorton.)

"In the year 1650, the Baptist churches began to form themselves into Associations." (David Benedict, History of the Baptists, p. 304.)

"Associations.—the oldest American Baptists, the Philadelphia Association 1707." (William Cathcart, The Baptist Encyclopedia, I, 47.)

(ISAAC) "Backus' church, and many others, waited until they could be satisfied that the Association did not assume any jurisdiction over the churches, before joining, and they now joined upon the express condition that no complaint should ever be received by the Association against any particular church that was not of the Association." (A.H. Newman, History of the Baptist Churches in the United States, pp. 265-266.) (Remember the Beaver Association is the one who claimed to have first withdrawn from the Campbells et al, and they were never members of the Beaver Association, J.P. W.)

"No Association or Convention has the right to dictate to the local church." (Roy Mason, The Church That Jesus Built, p. 98.)

"The writer can easily remember when Baptist Associations were wont to close their sessions by celebrating the Lord's Supper, and this they did for years; but was it right because our fathers did it? Who will advocate this practice today, or what Association on this continent will presume to administer the Supper?... Fifty years our fathers were wont to advise the churches to send their licentiates to the Association to receive ordination, and it was wont to select a Presbytery, and between them ordain the ministers. But who will advocate so unscriptural a procedure now? Twenty five or thirty years ago, the overwhelming majority of our churches in the south would indorse a Campbellite, and alien immersion as valid." (J.R. Graves, Old Landmarkism: What Is It?., pp. 81-82.)

"Long Run Association met at New Castle, the 1st Friday in September, 1830. Pond Creek and Goose Creek churches... sought admission into the Association, without any written expressions of their faith. They were rejected." (J.H. Spencer, A History of the Kentucky Baptists, p. 639.)

"Baptist Associations are but annual gatherings for the benefit of the churches, without any power of discipline or legislation." (David Benedict, Fifty Years Among the Baptists, p. 165.)

"...wherever such bodies attempt to interfere in the internal concerns of churches, they usurp a power which ought not to be conceded to them, and become a curse instead of a blessing." (Theology and History, Alin. Central Union Assoc., Penn., 1832, p. 6.)

"Air. (J.R.) Graves, in the standing column of the Baptist, says: 'That a body of immersed believers is the highest ecclesiastical authority in the world, and the only tribunal for the trial of cases of discipline; that the acts of a church are of superior binding force over those of an Association... and no Association or Convention can impose a moral obligation upon the constituent parts composing them." (D.B. Ray, Baptist Church Succession, quoting J.R. Graves, p. 224.)

"As a mere spectator, I did, however, visit the Redstone Association in the fall of 1812. After a more particular acquaintance with some of the members and ministers of that connexion, the church of Brush Run did finally agree to unite with that association on the grounds that no terms of union or communion other than the Holy Scriptures should be required." (Alexander Campbell, Christian Baptist, p. 92.)

"As you know I have no faith in the divine right of Associations, yet, to shield me from such far-off and underhand attacks ... I and the church with which I am connected are in 'full communion' with the Mahoning Baptist Association, Ohio,... I do intend to continue in connexion with this people so long as they will permit me to say what I believe, to teach what I am assured of, and to censure what is amiss in their views or practices. I have no idea of adding to the catalog of new sects." (Alexander Campbell, Christian Baptist, p. 217.)

"He (Alexander Campbell, J.P. W.) sought membership of his church in the Redstone Baptist Association." (Dr. D.N. Jackson, ed. American Baptist, November 23, 1942.)

"In addition to his acquaintance with Messrs. Luce and Speers, Mr. Campbell had, from time to time, formed that of other members belonging to the (Redstone) Association, who often urged that the Brush Run church should connect itself with this religious body... obstacle was, that the churches composing the association had adopted the Confession of Faith set forth by a Baptist Association at Philadelphia, September 25, 1747,... Upon these points, however, and upon the circumstance which led to a conditional union with the Red Stone Association during the fall of 1813,... They all pressed us to join their Redstone Association... exhibiting our remonstrance against all human creeds... express a willingness, upon certain conditions, to cooperate or to unite with that Association, provided always that we should be allowed to teach and preach whatever we learned from the Holy Scriptures, regardless of any creed or formula in Christendom. ... The proposition was discussed at the Association, and, after much debate, was decided by a considerable majority in favor of our being received. Thus a union was formed... We boldly urged for the Bible, for the New Testament Christianity." (Richardson, Memoirs of Campbell, I, 440-441.)

"Refusal to subscribe to any confession of faith in uniting with the Association, were not pleasing to a few active ministers. The Redstone Association of churches had adopted the Philadelphia Confession. To this Mr. Campbell would not subscribe or allow his associates to subscribe." (Gates and Hulbert, The Early Relations and Separation of Baptist and Disciples, p. 20.)

"The next meeting for the Red Stone Association was at hand. It met August 30, 1816, at Cross Creek. Mr. Campbell came as a messenger from the Brush Run church. At these meetings the various preachers present, whom the people desired to hear, were put on the program for sermons. More than any other preacher in the Association the people were eager to hear Mr. Campbell, and he was put on the program... He preached from the passage in Rom. 8:3, the famous Sermon on the Law, which created such excitement subsequently in the Baptist community... This sermon was a complete exposition of the views he had adopted as early as 1812 on the relation of the two covenants... The relation between them and the Association began already to be somewhat strained and formal." (Gates and Hulbert, The Early Relations and Separation of Baptists and Disciples, pp. 28, 29.)

"On the 30th day of August, 1820, a little more than two months after the Walker debate, the messengers appointed by the churches met and constituted the 'Mahoning Baptist Association.' In the spring of 1821, Mr. Bentley obtained a copy of the published Walker debate, with which he was highly pleased; and learning that the Redstone Association was opposed to Mr. Campbell and was endeavoring to injure him, he said to his friends that, in his opinion, Mr. Campbell had done more for the Baptists than any man in the West." (Richardson, Memoirs of Campbell, II, 44.)

"As he had been occasionally pressed by Elder Bentley to leave the Redstone Association and unite with the Mahoning, and as a number of the members of the Brush Run church lived in Wellsburg and its vicinity, he concluded to form there a separate congregation in which he would have his membership, and which might afterwards unite with the Mahoning Association." (Ibid., II, 68-69.)

"...we have dismissed the following brethren in good standing with us, to constitute a church of Christ at Wellsburg,... Done at our meeting, August 31st A.D. 1823, and signed by order of the church. Thomas Campbell." (Richardson, Memoirs of Campbell, footnote, Vol. II, p. 69.1

"The first Baptist Association to be controlled by the Reformers was the Mahoning of Ohio....

This Association met with the Reformer's church at Sharon, August, 1829, just after a division in the Baptist church. A list of the sixteen churches composing the Association indicates that the Baptist element had been completely lost by 1827. This Association was dissolved in 1830 without a discerning vote, as far as its Baptist form was concerned. Along with the Mahoning, and almost as early to abandon its creeds and constitution, was the Stillwater Association of Ohio." (Gates and Hulbert, The Early Relations and Separation of Baptists and Disciples, pp. 68-69.)

"The year (1829), passed by and the Association met, as it proved, for the last time as an ecclesiastical body, at Austintown... The action taken at Austintown may be regarded as the formal separation from the Baptists:..." (Life of Walter Scott, by Wm. Baxter, pp. 91-92.)

"The following query was sent up to a small Association in the state of (Kentucky) for an answer: 'What must a church do with her preacher who has embraced Campbellism?' To which the Association in her wisdom replied, 'As we know not what Campbellism is, we cannot tell her what io do.'" (A.W. Fortune, The Disciples in Kentucky, p. 76.)

"During the year 1830, which was pre-eminently the year of separation of Baptists from Reformers, reports are numerous and dark of the state of affairs in Baptist churches... The following lamentation is taken from a report of the state of things in Tennessee by Mr. McConnico: 'My beloved brethren:—Campbellism has carried away many whom I thought firm. These wandering stars and clouds without water ever learning and never able to come to the knowledge of the truth, make proselytes much more the children of the devil than they were before. O Lord! hear the cries and see the tears of the Baptists; for Alexander hath done them much harm." (Early Relations and Separation of Baptists and Disciples p. 100.)

"The church to which Andrew Broadus ministered was the next to take similar action. A conference was agreed upon, to which eight churches sent committees or delegates. They met at Upper King and Queen meeting-house, Dec. 30, 1830... set forth in the report as follows: 'The system of religion known by the name of Campbellism has spread of late among our churches to a distressing extent, and seems to call loudly for remedial measures... Resolved, That this conference recommend to the churches the observation of a day of solemn humiliation, with fasting and prayer, with reference to the state of religion and the distress which has given rise to this meeting. Accordingly, Tuesday, the 8th of March, was appointed for the purpose'." (Separat. of Bap. & Discip., p. 95-97.)

APPENDIX

Since the Baptists try to trace their church succession, and since they do that by claiming that only their own baptism is genuine, therefore it is a clear gone conclusion that they must also trace their baptism to prove their church succession. Succession is their main reason for depending upon and arguing from a historical standpoint so much. And, of course, some people reason that since you CAN trace their church succession, together with their baptism back to the Lord, or John the Immerser, they must be right. However, they do not investigate the historical issues; but take for granted that they are truthful and therefore they thus get many "joiners." Because of that, I am offering this appendix on baptism. In this I shall show that they are not right on baptism, and have never been right on it as a church, although many of their men, the real scholars among them do, to save their scholarly reputation acknowledge the truth on baptism, as here I show.

"Mankind are prone to two evil intellectual habits: one is to look at only one side of a question, and the other is to carry the partial view thus obtained to an extreme. No where are these unfortunate tendencies more conspicuous than in the domain of religion, and on no subject, perhaps, more than on the subject of baptism." (Rev. H.H. Tucker, "Baptist Doctrines," ed. Rev. Charles A. Jenkins, 1880, p. 173.)

"God's law is a unit; God's law is virtually himself; it is himself expressed. To speak lightly of IT is to speak lightly of HIM; and to say that any thing he has commanded is simply a form, a MERE form, a naked form, and NOTHING BUT a form, would seem to be shocking irreverence." (Ibid., p. 176.)

"But baptism ... is the public putting on of Christ;... Putting on Christ is what an angel cannot do. It is what cannot be done in heaven; in no part of the universe except on

EARTH can this glorious deed be done... Baptism is an expression, brief but comprehensive, of the leading doctrines of the New Testament. ... It is itself the word of God. ... Is it conceivable that the great God could possibly lend the sanction of his authority to that which is nothing but emptiness? or that he would command us to do that which might well be left undone?" (Ibid., pp. 179-180.)

"Hear Dr. Lofton, Brother Moody's moderator... He says. 'Baptism, ordinarily, is inseparable from salvation by faith, since obedience to the first command of Christ is inseparable from faith.'" (Harding-Moody Debate, May, 1889, p. 284.)

"Baptism is a ritualistic or ceremonial act by which one is received into the membership of the church. It is an essential qualification since there can be no membership in a church without being baptized. ... As Dr. Pendleton has well said, 'The believer's first public act of obedience is baptism.' One cannot follow Christ, or obey him without going down into the water of baptism. And the statement is here ventured that no service of a believer is acceptable to Christ until this first public- declarative act is performed." (Dr. J.E. Cobb, New Manual for Baptist Churches, 1941_2 p. 39.)

"Baptism is commanded, and Faith obeys because it is commanded, and thus takes her proper place." (C.H. Spurgeon, Baptismal Regeneration," Baptist Doctrines, p. 147.)

"Baptism is also FAITH TAKING HER PROPER PLACE." (Ibid., p. 146.)

"This is faith, receiving of the truth of Christ: first knowing it to be true, then acting upon that belief... Now that such a flaith as this should save the soul, is, I believe, reasonable; yea, more, it is certain." (Ibid., pp. 140-141.)

"If we do not understand the commission, it is not at all likely that we shall discharge it aright. To alter these words were more than impertinence: it would involve the crime of treason against the authority of Christ and the best interests of the souls of men." (Ibid., p. 116.)

"Acts 2:37-41. This was the first baptism after the descent of the Spirit. It is a key to the Comforter's interpretation of the Saviour's great commission, as he directed the proceedings of the inspired apostles." (William Cathcart, Baptist Doctrines, p. 74.)

"Gospel truth is the means through which the new life comes to the soul... But this truth is from God, and endures forever. There is no salvation but in conformity to it. Rom. 2:8; 2 Thess. 1:7-8." (Rev. E.G. Taylor, Baptist Doctrines, p. 535.)

"When the Holy Spirit distinguished the day of Pentecost with the overwhelming display of his regenerating grace, all those who repented under his influence were baptized, and the work of the Spirit began, as the work of Christ had begun, in the observance of this rite. The New Testament often speaks of baptism in such an emphatic manner as almost to identify it with the work of God in the soul, of which it is a symbol, that is, with spiritual washing, with death to sin and resurrection from it, and with the removal of guilt by pardon, Jno. 3:5; Acts 22:16; Tit. 3:5; 1 Pet. 3:21. If we find any difficulty with these expressions, is it not because we have accustomed ourselves to regard baptism a mere ceremony, a vague emblem, setting forth certain indefinite phases of the divine life, but not ministering nourishment to it? Thus in every way the New Testament affirms the importance of baptism, and does so even at the risk of creating the impression in some minds that the rite contains an occult spiritual power to save the soul, a danger which the Holy Spirit of inspiration evidently deemed less hurtful than that of undervaluing the ordinance." (J.B. Jeter, Baptist Principles Reset, article by Franklin Johnson, pp. 192-193.)

"But it is said that the Greek preposition, EIS, translated INTO, means TO, and that Philip and the eunuch only went TO the water... He knows, also, that EIS is translated INTO, in all these places, (Acts 8:11, 12, 13, 14, 20, 21, 22, and 38.)... This little word EIS, is a strange word, indeed, if what they say of it, is true. It will take a man INTO a country, INTO a city, INTO a house, INTO a ship, INTO heaven, INTO hell—INTO any place in the universe, except the water! Poor word! afflicted, it seems, with hydrophobia." (J.M. Pendleton, Three Reasons Why I Am A Baptist, pp. 120-121.)

"The apostles were, on that memorable day (Pentecost), copiously imbued with the Holy Spirit—they were baptized in the Spirit—they were endued with power from on high. All things whatsoever Jesus had said to them were brought to their remembrance. They were required for the first time to show their understanding of the commission of their ascended Lord. How did they understand it? How did they execute it? First, the gospel was preached. (He then quotes Acts 2:38.)... No one contends that the command, 'Repent,' is applicable to infants, and it is certain that the injunction, 'Be baptized,' has no reference to them; for it is as clear as the sun in heaven that the same persons are commanded to repent and be baptized." (J.M. Pendleton, Ibid., pp. 19-20.)

"The ordinary meaning of EN is IN, and of EIS, INTO." (Ibid., p. 138.)

"He baptized them EIS (because of or with reference to) repentance, just as Peter demanded in Acts 2:38." (Dr. D.N. Jackson (debate with Roy Cogdill, Am. Bap. 12/15/48.) "Docs Jno. 5:25 reveal the complete plan of salvation? It does, and so does Acts 2:38." (Ibid., Jan. 1, 1949.)

Thayer teaches eis expresses the end aimed at and secured by repentance and baptism, just previously enjoined. (Thayer, Greek-English Lexicon, p. 94.)

"My friend claims that EIS in Acts 2:38 means IN ORDER TO, SO DO I." (Dr. L.S. Ballard, Ballard-Borden Debate, 1914, p. 97.)

"IN ORDER TO THE FORGIVENESS OF SINS (Matt. 26:28; Luke 3:3) we connect naturally with both the preceding verbs. This clause states the motive or object which should induce them to repent and be baptized. It enforces the entire exhortation, not one part of it to the exclusion of the other... Repentance and the first fruits of repentance were generally inseparable. The former could not be genuine without manifesting itself in the latter." (Hovey's American Commentary, IV, 53.)

"They may happen to be right on EIS, your witness puts it that way." (Ben M. Bogard, Bogard- Hardeman Debate, 1938, p. 132.)

"Those who repented of their sins should be dipped, baptized, 'unto remission of sins'; that is, that they might enter in and have part in that final- really-atoning sacrifice." (J.B. Jeter, Baptist Principles Reset, article by Howard Osgood, p. 181.)

"'Brothers, what shall we do?' Peter said to them, 'You must repent, and every one of you be baptized in the name of Jesus Christ, in order to have your sins forgiven; then you will receive the gift of the Holy Spirit.'" (Acts 2:38, Edgar J. Goodspeed's Version.)

"'Brothers, what shall we do?' Peter said to them, 'You must repent—and, as an expression of it, let every one of you be baptized in the name of Jesus Christ—that you may have your sins forgiven; and then you will receive the gift of the Holy Spirit.'" (Acts 2:38, Charles B. William's Version.)

"The term salvation ... is commenced in repentance, carried forward in sanctification, and will be completed by the resurrection from the dead. The sincere believer in Christ, even before baptism, is in a state of salvation, but his salvation is incomplete. Now, God saves us by all the means which he employs to instruct, impress, purify, and preserve us. The written word, the ministry of the word, meditation, prayer, baptism, the Lord's Supper, afflictions, are all means by which God saves us." (J.B. Jeter, Campbellism Examined, 1855, p. 275.)

"That there should have been unbaptized disciples at Troas or anywhere else in the apostolic age is so contrary to all that is recorded as to be incredible." (H.C. Vedder, Dawn of Christianity, 1894, p. 124.)

"Good old Du Veil, who found his way from Judiasm, through Romanism and Anglicanism to the Baptist position, says in his Commentary on the Acts, London, 1685, (2:38), 'IN THE REMISSION OE SINS,'... He confounded the use of EIS with that of EN, according to the imperfect grammar of those days; but he had not heard of 'on account of,' as a translation of EIS." (J.W. Wilmarth, Footnote in "Baptist Quarterly," Julv 1877, p. 320.)

From 1835-39, Silas E. Shepherd edited the "Primitive Christianity" in Auburn, Cayuga County, N.Y."In 1836 volume under the factious title, 'Campbellism About A Century Ago,' he published an 'Extract from a serious Reply to the Rev. John Wesley, by Gilbert Boyce, a Baptist,' which we transcribe in full. (Let it be noted that it has now been over two hundred years since these words of Boyce were penned)...' (Acts 2:38). It ought to be observed that remission of sins is not promised to repentance only, but to repentance and baptism... Therefore, it appears plain that baptism is to be an inseparable companion with repentance, as faith is to be with them both, in order to receive the promise. If any man will be so venturous as to cast out baptism from the above text, and declare remission of sins to repentance only, I may by the same authority he can produce, cast out repentance, and declare remission of sins to baptism only... Do you know of any man who lived in the apostle's day who received remission of sins, etc., before he believed, repented and was baptized?" (Guy N. Woods, Firm Foundation, May 16, 1939, quotation from Baptist paper.) Thus we see the Baptist, about 1736, taught Acts 2:38 just as we teach it today.

"That baptism is FOR the remission of sins none will deny. But the import of the passage turns on the force of the term 'FOR.' In the Greek the preposition EIS is used. Every scholar knows, and every intelligent reader may learn from unquestionable authority, that it bears in the New Testament various meanings. It is sometimes, but rarely, rendered FOR, in the sense of 'IN ORDER TO.' Its usual rendering is INTO." (J.B. Jeter, Campbellism Examined, 1855, p. 261-262.)

"Repent ye, and let every one of you be baptized in the name of Jesus Christ, for the remission of sins.' 'For remission of sins,' then, whatever may be its meaning, is stated as a reason for the latter command (BAPTISM, J.P. W.) and not the former. The command to repent is given imperatively, without a reason—Repent YE. There was reason enough for this found in their conscious guilt and consequent alarm. But the reason why they should be baptized in the name of Jesus Christ is not so apparent, hence a reason is given: 'For the remission of sins.'" (A.P. Williams, "An Examination of Lard's Review of Jeter," p. 302- 303.)

"The primary meaning of the Greek word here rendered 'for,' is 'into,' so that the passage properly reads, 'Repent and be baptized every one of you INTO, or unto, the remission of sins." (Crawford, Crawford-Sweeny Debate, held in Springfield, Elgin Country, Ontario, Canada, 1874, p. 231.)

"With the preposition into before the name of the element into which an object is plunged or immersed, expressing fully the act of passing from one element into another." (T.J. Conant, Baptize in, pub. by American Bible Union, 1861, p. 91.)

"O strange and wonderful transaction!" he says of baptism. (Ibid., p. 103.)

"BE BAPTIZED... (not IN ORDER TO, but) ON ACCOUNT OF REMISSION OF SIN. That is, because your sins have been remitted. To this view there are insuperable objections. First. It puts an unauthorized sense upon the preposition EIS. 'On account of' is not one of the recognized meanings of EIS. No Greek would have employed the phrase here used to express the idea of ON ACCOUNT OF AN (accomplished) REMISSION. Another preposition would have been used, DIA OR PERI, for example. ... If Peter had meant IN ORDER TO DECLARE OR PROFESS REMISSION, he would have said so. As he did not, what right have we to insert here a word or an idea of which there is not the slightest trace in his language? ... 'In order to declare (or symbolize)' would be a monstrous translation of EIS;... But the natural construction connects the latter with both the preceding verbs... They ask 'What shall we do?' i.e., in order to be forgiven. He replies by telling them to repent and be baptized." (J.W. Wilmarth, Baptist Quarterly, July 1877, pp. 302-303.)

Referring to being baptized on account of the remission of sins, he said: "This interpretation was doubtless suggested, and is now defended, on purely dogmatic grounds. It is feared that if we give to EIS its natural and obvious meaning, undue importance will be ascribed to baptism, the atonement will be undervalued, and the work of the Holy Spirit disparaged. Especially it is asserted that here is the vital issue between Baptists and Campbellites. We are gravely told that if we render EIS in Acts 2:38 IN ORDER TO, we give up the battle, and must forthwith become Campbellites; whereas if we translate it ON ACCOUNT OF, or IN TOKEN OF, it will yet be possible for us to remain Baptists." (Ibid., p. 304.)

"Such methods of interpretation are unworthy of Christian scholars... And as to Campbellism, that spectre which haunts many good men and terrifies them into a good deal of bad interpretation, shall we gain any thing by maintaining a false translation and allowing the Campbellites to be champions of the true, with the world's scholarship on their side, as against us? Whoever carries the weight of our controversy with the Campbellites UPON THE EIS WILL

BREAK THROUGH—there is no footing there for the evolution of the theological skater. Shall we never learn that truth has nothing to fear from a true interpretation of any part of God's word, and nothing to gain by a false one? The truth wifi suffer nothing by giving to EIS its true signification. When the Campbellite translates IN ORDER TO in Acts 2:38, they translate correctly. Is a translation false because the Campbellites endorse it?" (Ibid. pp. 304-305.)

"Acts 2:38, is a very important passage—the key-note of the New Testament teaching as to obedience of the gospel." (Ibid. p. 306.)

In March, 1949, I debated with Dr. D.N. Jackson in his then home, Laurel, Miss., during which he answered a statement in Writing which I still have wherein I asked, "The Greek word eis, in Acts 2:38, translated 'for' in the King James version of the Bible, means 'because of.'" D'. Jackson added "or with reference to" and signed it. Thus you can see the down-right prejudice against the plain truth of the Bible.

"I protested in my opening speech that I did not believe baptism was because of remission." (J.B. Moody, Moody-Harding Debate, 1889, p. 327.)

"Those words which have caused so much controversy must be construed with deesou Christouf and not with 'be baptized.'... This view, presented above, is not new to me: ... It solves a difficult problem and removes the odium attached to the words 'baptism for the remission of sins.'" (Dr. L.S. Ballard, Ballard-Borden Debate, 1914, pp. 115-116.)

"ODIUM: 'OFFENSIVE; UNPOPULARITY: AS ODIUM OF TREASON. 2. FEELING OF EXTREME REPUGNANCE, OR DISLIKE AND DISGUST." (Funk-Wagnail, Vol. 2, 1710.) See the prejudice?

"The preposition m always governs the accusative case and therefore progressive in its application. It is translated into, unto or for. It can never mean in consequence of."

(Letter to the author from the Baptist Baylor University, January 7, 1942.)

"I have just examined a HALF DOZEN Greek Lexicons as to their discussion of eis, and I find NOT ONE giving any reference in Greek literature where it has a DISTINCTIVE RETROSPECTIVE MEANING;... (He then refers to Matt. 3:11 and 12:41 and says:) ... it is not necessarily RETROSPECTIVE but may BE IN REALITY PROSPECTIVE. So I feel from lexical authority you have been taught properly 'that it is always prospective.'... RETROSPECTIVE VIEW in Acts 2:38, ... I do not endorse such a view, and feel it weakens the Baptist position to meet the Campbellites with such a WEAK ARGUMENT of a single DOUBTFUL TEXT." (Letter to the author from Charles B. Williams, Baptist Greek Professor for 38 years, dated at Shilo, N.C., January 14, 1942.) (His Caps, J.P. W.)

"Normally eis looks forward and I know of no case in the N.T. where it looks back. You will find in Thayer's Lexicon under eis II 2ba, these meanings: for, for the benefit of, to the advantage of; see Eph. 1:19 and 3:2; 2 Cor. 13:4; Col. 1:25. These are not 'retrospective' but they are akin to "because off 'on account of' with a forward look. Again in Thayer II 2d, many examples are given of eis meaning with respect to, in reference to, as regards, forward looking, of course." (Letter to the author from D.A. Penick, Prof, of Classical Language, University of Texas, January 10, 1942.) (His Emphasis, J.P. W.)

"As far as 1 know, the Greek preposition EIS always precedes its object. I do not find that lexicons or grammars of New Testament Greek recognize 'because of' or 'on account of' as one of the meanings of EIS." (Letter to the author from Alan D. McKillop, Department of English, Rice Institute, Houston, Texas, January 17, 1942. His Caps, J.P. W.)

"The word 'EIS' in Acts 2:38 of the Greek Edition of the Bible really seems very clear. It is defined in Greek dictionaries 'direction towards, in, or into.' ... You will notice that I have made no connection between the Greek word 'EIS' and your translations, which were 'with reference to' or 'because of.' We could find no connection therewith." (Letter to the author, from the Office of President James C. Morehead, Jr., Asst, to President, Rice Institute, Houston, Texas, January 1950.)

"You suggest that EIS may mean 'because of,' but I doubt it. I never observed such a meaning for it ... a sense the Greek could not possibly bear." (Letter to Basil Holt, from Edgar J. Goodspeed, N.T.translator, Los Angeles, California, May 7, 1940 and published in the Gospel Advocate, June 25, 1942.)

"It is evident from the narrative of Acts 16 and 18 that he did preach baptism, at Corinth and elsewhere, as a part of the gospel." (J.W. Wilmarth, Baptism and Remission, Baptist Quarterly, July, 1877, p. 312.)

"Without controversy, by baptism God separates the believer from the world." (J.W. Wilmarth, Baptist Quarterly, July 1877, p. 317.)

"In those early days baptism swiftly followed that which it expressed, closely conjoined with repentance and faith in time as well as in teaching, so that little opportunity was given for the question, What is the status of an unbaptized believer?" (Ibid., p. 314.)

"Does not the close connection of the Spirit's work with baptism in John 3:5 and Titus 3:5, indicate that a work is wrought upon the believer, as well as that he performs a work himself? And may not this be the completion of the whole process of the 'new birth'?" (Ibid., p. 318.)

JOHN'S BAPTISM NOT THE SAME AS OUR BAPTISM

"Christian baptism was instituted by Christ, when he submitted to John's baptism, adopting its form, with some change of meaning." (Edward T. Hiscox, Baptist Directory,

p. 121.)

"It has been a question respecting the baptism of John, whether it was the same as the ordinance instituted by Christ, (Matt. 28:19) and observed in the church in all ages since. We are decidedly of the opinion that it was not the same, but merely an introductory rite, designed to prepare the way for the gospel dispensation; and in this we agree, not only with the ancient church, but with the most respectable writers, Baptists and Pedobaptists, of the present day... This baptism took place under the JEWISH DISPENSATION. ... Our Saviour lived under the old dispensation, and was a strict observer of the institutions of Moses;... Christian baptism originated in the express command of Christ: 'Go ye and teach all nations, baptizing them in the name of the Father, and of the Son, and of the Holy Ghost.' No such origin can be claimed for the baptism of John, who baptized for some time BEFORE HE KNEW CHRIST, John 1:31. He ascribes his commission to the FATHER, John 1:33. The baptism of John was EVIDENTLY a preparatory ordinance... The baptism of John, unlike Christian baptism, was not administered in the name of the Father, of the Son, and the Holy Ghost. Acts 19:2. Indeed, John did not baptize in the name of Christ, or in any other name; but merely directed those who came to his baptism to 'believe on him who should come after him,' Acts 19:4." (J. Newton Brown, Baptist Encyclopedia of Religions Knowledge, pp. 177-178.)

"His commission to the apostles, and to all succeeding ministers,... The Baptists,... believe that the ordinance of baptism is positively binding on every Christian who has the opportunity to observe it. They believe it to be essential to salvation, in the same sense that obedience to any other command of the Saviour is necessary to salvation... he who should deliberately refuse to be baptized, or to perform any other duty, so far as he understood that duty, and had the opportunity to perform it, would thus furnish evidence that he had not been born again, and consequently was unprepared for heaven ... we must obey the precepts exactly as it was meant to be observed; we have no right to deviate, in the slightest degree, from the prescribed rule, just as the Jews could not, without guilt, deviate from a strict compliance with the ceremonies of their law." (Ibid., p. 181.)

"Hear Dr. Loftin, Brother Moody's moderator... He said: 'Baptism, ordinarily, is inseparable from salvation by faith, since obedience to the first command of Christ is inseparable from faith.'" (Harding-Moody Debate, May 1889, p. 284.)

"Baptism is a ritualistic or ceremonial act by which one is received into the membership of a church. It is an essential qualification since there can be no membership in a church without being baptized. ... As Dr. Pendleton has well said, 'The believer's first public act of obedience is baptism.' One cannot follow Christ, or obey him without going down into the water of baptism. And the statement is here ventured that no service of a believer is acceptable to Christ until this first public declarative act is performed." (Dr. J.E. Cobb, New Manual For Baptist Churches, 1941, p. 39.)

"And thus it is as clear as the sun in his noontide glory, that while the Jewish church was supplied with its members by GENERATION, the Church of Christ is furnished with its members by REGENERATION." (His Caps, J.P. W.) (J.M. Pendleton, Three Reasons Why I Am A Baptist, 1853, p. 49.)

"Primitive believers were known as such by their baptism—not soldiers, not recognized as Christians, until baptized; and, without this, they would not have been recognized as disciples, or followers, or friends, of Christ." (J.R. Graves, The Relation of Baptism to Salvation, 1881, p. 43.)

"If you knew that you were going to the judgment tomorrow, and your salvation depended upon your being baptized as Christ was, and as he has commanded you to be, you would not be at a moment's loss; you would, this day, be 'buried with him by baptism'; you would be 'planted in the likeness of his death'; and yet you will not obey. Are you not, then, rebels against Christ, and consequently exposed to his wrath?... Do not fail to do it—do not refuse to do it, and still hope to be saved, for you have no right to hope for Salvation... Your flagrant and inexcusable neglect of divine law declares you the enemy of Christ... 'HE THAT BELIEVETH AND IS BAPTIZED SHALL BE SAVED.'" (J.R. Graves, Relations of Baptism and Salvation, 1881, pp. 54-56.)

"'Except a man be born of water and the Spirit he cannot enter into the kingdom of God.' Nine- tenths of the Christian family, living and dead, have applied these words of Jesus to baptism, the works of the Spirit, and the earthly church." (Wm. Cathcart in Baptist Doctrines, p. 85.)

WHO IS WHO IN HISTORICAL BRIEFS?

Alexander, Gross. Professor of Vanderbilt University.

Armitage, Thomas D.D., Baptist. (1819-1896.) He was one of the founders and presidents of the American Bible Union. "Dr. Armitage is a scholarly man, full of information, with a powerful intellect; one of the greatest preachers in the United States; regarded by many as the foremost man in the American pulpit." (Wm. Cathcart, Baptist Encyclopedia, I, 39-40.)

Baker, Helen Dow, Department of Latin and Greek, Hardin-Simmons University, Abilene, Tex.

Ballard, L.S., Baptist. A Baptist of renown, as a debater, and editor who has several books in circulation as well as a few published debates. He resides in Dallas, Texas.

Barr, Vernon, Baptist. A Baptist debater and editor who lives in Dallas, Texas.

Beardsley, Frank Grenville, Congregational Church. For a number of years he was Professor of Theology at Talladega Theological Seminary, and has been Chaplain of the Missouri Society, S.A. R., since 1925. He is a member of the American Society of Church Historians; American Numismatic Association, and author of several books.

Benedict, David, Baptist. He entered Brown University, where he graduated in 1806. Soon after he was ordained as pastor of the Baptist church in Pawtucket, R.I., where he remained for twenty- five years. During all this time he had been busy gathering from every part of the country, the materials out of which to form a comprehensive history of the Baptist denomination.

Bogard, Ben M., Baptist. Founder of the Missionary Baptist Institute of Little Rock, Ark., who wrote a number of small books some of which were on historical subjects, and who was also editor and founder of the Baptist Searchlight, a Baptist religious journal. He claimed to have had more debates than any man who ever lived or died. Several of his debates are now in book form.

Brewer, G.C., evangelist of the church of Christ. An editor who is well known and recognized among his brethren as a prolific writer for religious papers, and has written several books, some of them being used as reference books.

Brown, J. Newton, Baptist. Professor of Theology and Pastoral Relations in the New Hampton Institute, N.H. He was the editorial secretary of the Baptist Publication Society in 1849. He is the author of the little creed book, commonly adopted in newly organized Baptist churches known as "The New Hampshire Confession." He is editor of one of the valuable works of modern times, the "Encyclopedia of Religious Knowledge." (Wm. Cathcart, Encyclopedia, I, 146.)

Burrage, Henry S., Baptist. Graduated from Brown University in the class of 1861. He was connected with the Newton Theological Institute for six years. Editor and author of "A History of the Baptists in New England."

Campbell, Thomas. A Presbyterian preacher who came to America in 1807. He organized what was known as "The Christian Association." He accepted nothing but the Bible as his creed, which forced him to be an Independent. With his son and several others all of whom had read themselves into the belief that immersion was the one baptism, were immersed by a Baptist preacher in June, 1812, and was very popular among Baptists of that day. Some claim he started the Reformation movement (as it is called) in America when he made his famous "Declaration and Address," 1809.

Campbell, Alexander. The son of Thomas Campbell was educated at Glasgow University and came to America in 1809. Hurst, in his "Baptist History," says of him: "His personality was of the most vigorous type, and for over a generation his name was a tower of strength over the whole

United States." (page 557.) Had such noted characters as Henry Clay as his friends, and was invited to speak before the Congress of the United States, as well as to write a translation of the Book of Acts for the Baptist Version of the Bible. He was also a prolific debater.

Cathcart, William, Baptist. He received his literary and theological education in the University at Glasgow, Scotland, and in Horton, now Rowden College, Yorkshire, England. He came to the U.S.in 1853 and is the author of the "Baptist Encyclopedia," a two volume set of encyclopedias.

Cobb, J.E., Baptist. To my knowledge he is a prolific speaker, with a commanding voice and good personality. He has debated quite a bit, having had two oral debates with this writer as well as one lengthy published debate. He was a state man among the Baptists at that time, and is the author of a Baptist church Manual, of which Ben M. Bogard, D.D., said, "It is my opinion that it is the best Manual ever written." (Baptist Searchlight, Dec. 10, 1941.)

Conant, T.J., Baptist. Professor of Biblical Literature and Criticism in the Theological Seminary at Hamilton, N.Y.and the Rochester Seminary. Worked for a number of years with the Baptist American Bible Union. "In 1839 he prepared a translation of Gesenius's Hebrew grammar, which he has since enlarged and improved, and it is still the standard Hebrew grammar of the Schools in America and Europe. ... It is now admitted that he stands in the front rank of Oriental scholars." (Wm. Cathcart, Baptist Encyclopedia, 1, 261-262.)

Cramp, J.M., Baptist. He was born in England and most of his work was done in England and Canada. "Dr. Cramp's theology is sound, his labors have been abundant, and his influence and usefulness have been very great in the maritime provinces. He is also widely and favorably known in the United States." (Wm. Cathcart, Baptist Encyclopedia, I, 286.)

Crawford, John, Baptist. According to A.H. Newman's,

"Century of Baptist Achievements," page, 353, he was an educator and started the Prairie College, Rapid City, Manitoba and sacrificed considerably for it for five years. He is well spoken of as a faithful Baptist.

Davis, W.M., Christian Church. Author, and considered somewhat of an authority on church history, who wrote "How the Disciples Began and Grew," published by the Standard Pub. Co., Cincinnati, Ohio.

DeGroot, A.T., Baptist. Dean of Chapman College, Los Angeles, California. He wrote the tract, "Three-fourths of a Loaf," which was reprinted in a Baptist Historical Quarterly known as "The Chronicle."

Dosker, Henry, Presbyterian. Professor of Church History of the Presbyterian Seminary. Louisville, Kentucky, and author of several articles in the "International Bible Encyclopedia."

Erdman, Charles R., Presbyterian. Professor of Practical Theology in Princeton Theological University, Princeton, N.J., and author of articles appearing in the "International Bible Encyclopedia.'

Fausset, A.R., Church of England. Rector of St. Culberts, York, England, and joint author of the "Critical and Explanatory Commentary on the Bible," and compiler of the "Bible Cyclopedia.'

Fortune, Alonza Willard, Christian Church. Pastor of the Central Christian Church, Lexington, Ky., and author of at least three historical books. "The Disciples in Kentucky" is endorsed by such men as C.L. Pyatt, Chairman of the Faculty, The College of Bible; E.E. Snoddy, The College of the Bible.

Garner, Albert, Baptist. Dean of Texas Baptist Institute. "Dr. Garner is a scholar and prolific writer... and is the logical one to edit 'The Searchlight.'" (James F. Dew, "The Baptist Searchlight," edited by Ben Al. Bogard until his death.) Dr. Bogard himself says of Dr. Garner, "He is the BEST SCHOLAR IN TEXAS and just about everybody in that great state knows it." ("Baptist Searchlight," December 25, 1949.)

Goodspeed, Edgar J., Baptist. In the Baptist churches of importance he was known as a scholar and wonderful pastor. "In 1865 he was called to the Second Baptist Church, Chicago. There he began a pastorate of eleven years, during, which may be justly called a remarkable one ... he was tendered by the Home Mission Society the position of President of Benedict Institute, of Columbia, S.C." (Baptist Encyclopedia, I, 458.) He has for years lived in and been connected with the University of Chicago "The invitation of the University Press to provide such a translation was accepted by the present translator in the hope that it might result in a version with something of the ease, boldness, and unpretending vigor which marks the original Greek." This is to be found in his Version of the New Testament which he translated. (Preface, signed Edgar J. Goodspeed, The University of Chicago, August 3, 1923.)

Gates, Errett, Christian Church. Associate in Church History, University of Chicago, and joint author of "Relations and Separations of Baptists and Disciples."

Graves, J.R., Baptist. "In his nineteenth year he was elected principle of the Kingsville Academy, Ohio." He taught school for some time, "going over a college course without a teacher, mastering a modern language yearly." In 1846 he was elected editor of the "Tennessee Baptist." "It is difficult to give even a brief summary of the work accomplished and the influence exerted by a mind so active, an intellect so great, and a genius so uncommon... He is the acknowledged head of the great movement among Baptists known as 'Old Landmarkism.'" He is the author of several books, some of which are "Trilemma," "Old Landmarkism: What Is It?" and he wrote the Introduction to Orchard's, "Baptist History." These quotations are from William Cathcart's, "Baptist Encyclopedia." Here are other quotations about him: "One of the most learned Baptists of modern times... fully competent to speak as a historian." (Dr. J.E. Cobb, in a debate with the author, p. 20.) "That towering, outstanding character, the like of which has not been seen in American Baptist history, and we very much doubt, shall ever be seen again." (W.M. Nevins, "Alien Baptism and Baptists," p. 141.) The Georgia Governor said of him: "There is one man who has done more than any fifty men now living to enable the Baptists of America to know their own history and their own principles, and to make the world know them." (Cathcart, "Baptist Encyclopedia," I, 467-468.)

Hackett, H.B., Baptist. Author of a noted commentary of Acts about 1851 of which it is said "has been styled by Dr. Peabody, in the 'North American Review,' 'one of the very few works of the kind in the English language which approaches in point of massive erudition the master-works of the great German critics, differing from them only in possessing a soundness and accuracy which they sometimes lack.'" "He contributed thirty articles to Dr. Wm. Smith's 'Dictionary of the Bible'... and wrote an introduction to the American edition of Westcott's 'Introduction to the Study of Gospels,'" and other books. (Cathcart's, "Baptist Encyclopedia," I, 483.)

Haley, J.J., Christian Church. Author of "Makers and Molders of the Reformatory Movement."

Hardy, James B., Baptist. Defender of the faith of the Primitive or Regular Baptists. In the debate with Isham E. Wallace it is said of him: "Elder James B. Hardy, of Crittenden County, Kentucky, was selected to represent the Regular Baptists. The debatants met at Mount Moriah church, in Marshall County Kentucky, on Monday, July 26th, 1880, and the following pages contain an account of what there took place." (Preface of the debate.)

Harvey, Hezekiah, Baptist, "Born in Hulven, County of Suffolk, England, Nov. 27, 1821, and came to America in 1830. He was graduated from Madison University and

Hamilton Theological University Seminary in 1847." He taught in several colleges and Universities, and wrote some books one of which is called, "The Church." (Wm. Cathcart, "Baptist Encyclopedia," I, 507.)

Hiscox, Edward T., Baptist. "He is the author of 'The Baptist Church Director,'... 30,000 copies of which have been sold. It has been translated into six foreign languages, and is generally used by our foreign missionaries." He also wrote other books of note among Baptists including the "Standard Baptist Church Manual" with some 160,000 or more copies of this man's books being sold. (Quotations from Cathcart's and Hiscox's works, 528.)

Hovey, Alvah, Baptist. Born in Greene, Chenango County, N.Y., March 5th, 1820. He taught much and wrote for many papers as well as the author of a number of books, many of which were very greatly received by the reading public, among which was called "An American Commentary on the New Testament," of seven volumes.

Hulbert, Eri, Christian Church. He was dean of the Divinity School University of Chicago, supposed to be a member of the Christian Church. He is joint author of "The Early Relations and Separations of the Baptists and Disciples," published by the Century Co., Chicago.

Hurst, John F. Baptist. He wrote an excellent "Short History of the Christian Church," and is an excellent, fair and impartial writer.

Jackson, D.N., Baptist. He is a writer of small tracts and books including a historical work appearing in his paper the "American Baptist," which is claimed to be an old paper once edited by some of the leaders among this branch of Baptists; such as J.R. Graves, J.N. Flail, etc. He wrote "Ten Reasons Why I Am A Baptist," and has had many debates, two with the author, and is now considered to be the best debater among them today.

Jeter, J.B., Baptist. "About the close of the war he became the senior editor of the Religious Herald, and continued until his death, Feb. 10, 1880—"a period of fourteen years." He also wrote several books and tracts, some of which I have. Among them are, "Campbellism Examined," and "Baptist Principles Reset." "As a debater, he was ready, self-possessed, courteous, wisely conservative, added to which qualities were a force and ability that won universal attention." (Wm. Cathcart, "Baptist Encyclopedia," I, 601.)

Kesner, J.W., Baptist. He lives in Fort Smith, Ark., and has written some for religious (Baptist) papers, and a small book or two. He had one debate with Brother Ward Hogland, which was recorded and printed. He also has a small book which he is pleased to call "Campbellism Exposed," on which this writer challenged him, but he didn't see fit to accept. This book has extracts from others, noticeably Ben M. Bogard, and Vernon Barr, two other Baptists preachers. No Wonder Bogard said of it, "the like of which has not been seen before." (Searchlight, March 10, 1950.)

Kurtz, D.W., President of McPherson College, McPherson, Kansas and a noted historian.

Loftin, George Augustus, Baptist. He pastored, successfully, such places as Dalton, Ga., Memphis, Tenn., and St. Louis, Mo. "Besides many articles and sermons for the periodical press, he has written and published some bound volumes, which have received favorable criticism, and which indicates culture and originality... He was also president for two years of the Southern Baptist Publication Society, located at Memphis. Dr. Loftin is especially prominent and well known in the South, and he is rapidly acquiring a national reputation." (Cathcart, "Baptist Encyclopedia, II, 713-714.)

Martyr, Justin. One of the Ante-Nicene Fathers who died about 167 A.D., having seen some of the apostles.

Mason, Roy, Baptist. He is the author of a book called, "The Church That Jesus Built," besides some others. Perhaps this is his greatest work. It has an introductory by J.W.

Jent, Boliver, Mo., who is President (at that time) of Southwestern Baptist College. This book first appeared in 1923, and has been used as a text book in some Baptist Colleges. I have the seventh edition.

Matthews, Shaller, A Professor of Chicago University.

McGlothlin, W.J., Baptist. Professor of Church History in Southern Baptist Theological Seminary and has written a few books two of which are "Baptist Confessions of Faith," which was copyrighted in 1911; the other, "The Course of Christian History," 1918. He seems to have been a great man among the Baptists.

Milburn, J. H, Baptist. He was of considerable noteriety when he wrote his book, "Origin of Campbellism." He lived at Union City, Tenn., and wrote a number of other Baptist doctrinal books, and was quite a debater. He was editor of Baptist papers in his day.

Moody, J.B., Baptist. He was a recognized representative of Baptist doctrines, and had what has been considered one of the greatest debates ever conducted between Baptists and the church of Christ when he met J.A. Harding, at Nashville, Tenn., in May of 1889.

Morehead, James C. is the man who answered my letter, which answer is dated July 29, 1950. It came from the "Office of the President" of the Rice Institute, Houston, Texas and he was then "Assistant to the President" of that great school which is supposed to be unbiased in the matters discussed.

Mosheim, Johann Lorenz Von, Lutheran. He was a German Church historian of international note among all denominations, although he was a Lutheran. Born at Lubeck, Oct. 9, 1694 or 1695 and died Sept. 9, 1755. In the Preface of his "Ecclesiastical History," Dr. C. Coote said, "The fame of his literary ability diffused itself among all the nations of Christendom. The Danish Court invited him to Copenhagen, and rewarded his merit," as did many others. He is absolute authority among Church historians.

A Handbook of Historical Briefs

Neander, Johann Augustus Wilhelm, (Neander was self-chosen and means Greek, neos, new; aner, a man; hence, a Neander, after his conversion, is his reason.) He was born at Gottengen, Germany, January 16, 1789 and was Professor of Theology in the University of Berlin. "As a Christian scholar and thinker, he ranks among the first names in modern times," and his name is absolute authority. He wrote the "History of the Planting and Training of the Christian Church by the Apostles." (Preface of his book.)

Nelson, Wilbur, Baptist. Pastor of the Newport, R.I. Baptist church which bears the name, "First Baptist John Clarke Memorial Church" in honor of that great forerunner, Dr. John Clarke, whom a few claim was the originator of the first Baptist church in America. Nelson wrote a history of that church and its former pastor, Dr. Clarke. The book is called "The Hero of Aquidneck, a Life of Dr. John Clarke."

Nevin, W.M., Baptist. He wrote "Alien Baptism and the Baptists," which is an outgrowth of another book of request from the "State Mission Board of Kentucky." "Here is a book of real merit, written by the Rev. W.M. Nevin, who needs no introduction to Baptist people, he having been pastor of important churches in Kentucky, Texas, and Washington, D.C. He is a well-known Baptist minister." (Introduction of his book, by William Dudley Nowlin.)

Newman, Albert Henry, Baptist. Professor of several Baptist Colleges and Seminaries, including that of Baylor University, Waco, Texas. He is authority on church history. He is the author of several books, two of which are known as "A Century of Baptist Achievement," about 1901, and "A History of the Baptist Churches in the United States." "The highest estimate is placed upon his acquisitions and talents by competent judges who are familiar with his work." (Cathcart, "Baptist Encyclopedia, II, p. 839.)

Orchard, G.H., Baptist. He wrote "a concise History of

Foreign Baptists" with an introduction by J.R. Graves which is considered authentic by most people, but J.M. Cramp, another Baptist historian condemns it somewhat, in his history, pp. 99-100.

Paxton, J.F., Professor of the University of Oklahoma.

Peloubet's, "Bible Dictionary" is absolute authority.

Pendleton, J.M., Baptist. Pie was the pastor of the Bowling Green Kentucky Baptist Church for twenty years. He was Professor of Theology in Union University, Murfressboro, Tenn. and was almost a constant writer for church papers, and published several books, among them is his famous, "Three Reasons Why I Am a Baptist." His joint notes on the New Testament, and his "Baptist Church Manual," of which Ben M. Bogard said, "Pendleton's Manual, used by the great majority of the churches in America... Dr. Pendleton is considered one of the greatest scholars who ever lived, having read the Greek New Testament through thirty times. Dr. Pendleton wrote what we know as 'Pendleton's Manual,' the most widely used manual among Baptists. He also wrote many other books and is considered one of our greatest men." (Searchlight, December 10, 1949.) Dr. L.S. Ballard says of him, "Dr. J.M. Pendleton, an outstanding Baptist preacher, leader and teacher of his day, the man who wrote the "Church Manual" that was used as the doctrinal basis of all orthodox churches until recent years." (Dr. L.S. Ballard, "Election Made Plain," p. 68.)

Penick, D.A., Professor of Classical Languages, or was, when he wrote me a personal letter dated January 10, 1942, at the University of Texas, Austin, Texas; hence reputed to be unbiased on the matters therein discussed.

Potter, Lemuel, Primitive Baptist. He was a representative of the "Regular Old School (Primitive or Hardshell) Baptists who met W.P. Throgmorton, a Missionary Baptist in debate, at Fulton, Ky., for four days, beginning July 12, 1887, with a publication committee composed of J.N. Hall,

A Handbook of Historical Briefs

J.H. Milburn, Dr. H.C. Roberts and Dr. S.F. Cayce.

Ray, D.B., Baptist. He was editor of the "Baptist Sentinel," Lexington, Kentucky, "a man of marked ability and of great courage." (Cathcart's, "Baptist Encyclopedia," II, 409.) Later, he edited the "American Flag," which is now known as "American Baptist," and edited by Dr. D.N. Jackson, in Little Rock, Ark. "Not only as an evangelist is he known, but more as a debater on religious questions," says Mr. Cathcart in the Baptist Encyclopedia, II, 290. He wrote several books, but one of most importance, especially to this work, called "Baptist Succession."

Rayzor, James Newton, Baptist. He is the author of several books one of which is the "History of the Denton County (Texas) Baptist Association," which was published about 1936.

Richardson, Robert, a member of the church of Christ who was a physician and associate editor of the "Harbinger," and who also wrote the best and most widely read story of the life of Alexander Campbell, called "Memoirs of Alexander Campbell," in two massive volumes.

Robinson, H. Wheeler, Baptist. He wrote "The Life and Faith of the Baptists," from London, N.W.8 in which it is said, "Dr. Robinson reveals the origin and principles of the Baptists;... and fairly appraises the Baptist contributions to the Universal Church." Principle of Regents Park College; President of the Baptist Historical Society.

Rowe, John F., a great writer of the church of Christ, and whose descendants have followed in his foot-steps in that respect some of whom we still know. He wrote a historical work of considerable worth that was called "History of Reformatory Movements," about 1889.

Schaff, Philip. A great and influential writer who was born at Coire, Switzerland, Jan. 1, 1819. He attended universities in Tubingen, Halle, Berlin. He was one of the founders of the American Church of the Evangelical Alliance, and was president of the American Bible Revision

Committee. His books are so numerous that we haven't space to mention all of them. He wrote two church histories, "A Companion to the Greek Testament and the English Version," "Bible Dictionaries," and some Commentaries, and helped edit the "Religious Encyclopedia."

Scofield, C.I., Baptist. Author of what is called the "Scofield Bible," which contains his notes. He has also written other works, one in particular, a pamphlet called, "Rightly Dividing the Word of Truth."

Shepherd, Silas E., a member of the church of Christ who edited a paper at "Auburn, Cayuga County, N.Y.," in which he gives an extract from the pen of Gilbert Boyce, a Baptist, where he argues with "Rev. John Wesley, Methodist, which, according to Shepherd's paper, took place long before, and was titled, "Campbellism About A Century Ago," which would make it from that date, 1836, about 1736—a long time before Alexander Campbell's father was even born. Printed from the "Firm Foundation," May 16, 1939, by Guy N. Woods, a reliable member of the church of Christ.

Smith, William, author of the well-known "Smith's Bible Dictionary."

Spencer, J.T, Baptist. A Baptist historian who wrote, "A History of Kentucky Baptists," about 1885, which is a welcomed history to most people.

Spurgeon, C.H., Baptist. He was one of the greatest men of all ages in the Baptist church. "From London his fame spread throughout the land... Invitations to preach flowed in upon him from all quarters,... preaching in the Music Hall of the Surrey Gardens, an immense building, which, although capable of seating 7000, was always densely crowded... Week after week for upward of twenty-five years a sermon by Mr. Spurgeon had been published and not a few of them have had a remarkable sale. They have been translated into several languages, and their entire circulation is probably unparalleled." (Cathcart, "Baptist

Encyclopedia," II, 1094-1095.)

Thayer, Joseph Henry, "Professor of New Testament Criticism and Interpretation in the Divinity School of Harvard University," who wrote what is well considered the best Greek English Lexicon we have today.

Taylor, E.G., Baptist. He is placed among such eminent Baptist preachers as J.P. Boyce, Armitage, Jeter, Hovey, etc., so I consider him one of their greatest men, as he has an extended article on "Regeneration Essential to Salvation." (Information from the book called "Baptist Doctrines," p. 521.)

Throgmorton, W.P., Missionary Baptist. He was called as a representative of the Missionary Baptists in debate between them and the Primitive Baptists at Fulton, Ky., in July, 1887; meeting Lemuel Potter, with such men as J.N. Hall and J.H. Milburn, as helpers.

Tucker, H.H., Baptist. "...edited the "Christian Index," and perhaps the most brilliant Baptist Georgia has produced, ... In 1866, he was unanimously elected president of Mercer University... A remarkable sermon of his on 'Baptism,' preached at Saratoga in 1879, was published by the American Baptist Publication Society, and commanded very general attention because of its originality... Dr. Tucker's style of writing is polished and scholarly, racy, manly, pungent, and strongly Saxon, and, like his thoughts, logical and lucid. It never wearies, but always enchants and sparkles. His manner of speaking is bold, candid, and fearless. He is a logician by nature as well as by culture." (Cathcart's "Baptist Encyclopedia," II, 1171.)

Vedder, H.C., Baptist. He was a noted historian, and wrote what he called, "A Short History of the Baptists," which had several editions. He also wrote what is known as "The Dawn of Christianity." He was, at one time, the head of the Crozier Theological Seminary.

Wallace, Isham, Baptist. He represented the Missionary Baptists in debate with one James B. Hardy, a Regular, or

Primitive, sometimes called Hardshell Baptist, at Mt. Moriah Church, in Marshall County, Kentucky, July, 1880. This debate was put into book form.

Wallace, Dr. L.T., Department of Bible and Greek, Oklahoma Baptist University.

Ware, Charles Crossfield, Christian church. He was of Wilson, North Carolina, and in July of 1932 he put out a book on the life of Barton W. Stone which contains much history of worth.

Warlick, Joe S., who is known as a trail blazer for the church of Christ, and is one of the greatest debaters of all men. He possibly debated with more people, including women, than any other man of the church of Christ. He was also an editor, and published several books, and helps. In his debates, he seemed to know the other man's arguments before he made them, hence he never used a note book to follow, but was able to remember accurately everything in derail to the satisfaction of his brethren and to the defeat of his opponent. He was a great man in his field.

Whitsitt, William Heath, Baptist. He was a prolific writer in papers and books, among them is "A Question in Baptist History," about 1898. He was Professor of Biblical Introduction and Ecclesiastical History in the Southern Baptist Theological Seminary, and was born near Nashville, Tennessee, Nov. 25, 1841.

Wilhite, J, Porter, member of the church of Christ, and compiler of this and some other books and publications of debates.

Wilmarth, James W., Baptist. "...was born in Paris, France of American parents, in 1835... he gave time and toil to the ancient languages, and his heart to theological acquisitions, and at an early period in his life he was a scholarly preacher, well skilled in divinity... His articles on 'The Future Life,' and 'Baptism and Remission' in the "Baptist Quarterly, showed much originality, and produced a profound impression upon cultured men of God. No one stands higher in the estimation of his friends, and all who know him may be reckoned among the number. His position on any subject is very decided; he knew nothing of half-heartedness; his thoughts are as transparent as sunbeams. He shuns no responsibility in defending any truth; he avoids no sacrifice in assisting a friend. He is an able preacher, with a noble intellect, ardent piety, and a bright earthly future, if his slender frame will permit him to stay on earth for a few years." (Wm. Cathcart, "Baptist Encyclopedia," II, 1256.)

www.ingramcontent.com/pod-product-compliance
Lightning Source LLC
Chambersburg PA
CBHW060816050426
42449CB00008B/1678